Swearing N' Coloring
Special Edition

A Collection of Three Swear Word Adult Coloring Books

By
Swearing N' Coloring

Swearing N' Coloring Special Edition
A Collection of Three Swear Word Adult Coloring Books
Copyright 2016 by Don Cummings

ISBN-13: 978-1530791163
ISBN-10: 1530791162

Three Swearing N' Coloring Books In One!

F*ck Off! I'm Coloring
(F*ck Off! I'm Coloring Volume One)

I Love to F*cking Color!
(F*ck Off! I'm Coloring Volume Two)

I May Go to Hell, But I'll be Coloring on the Way Down!

73 Unique Designs!

Swear Words On Every Design!

One-Sided Designs To Prevent Bleed-Through!

Hours Of Relaxation!

Use Your Own Coloring Tools!
Crayons, Colored Pencils, Or Markers!

Get Fucking Started Today!

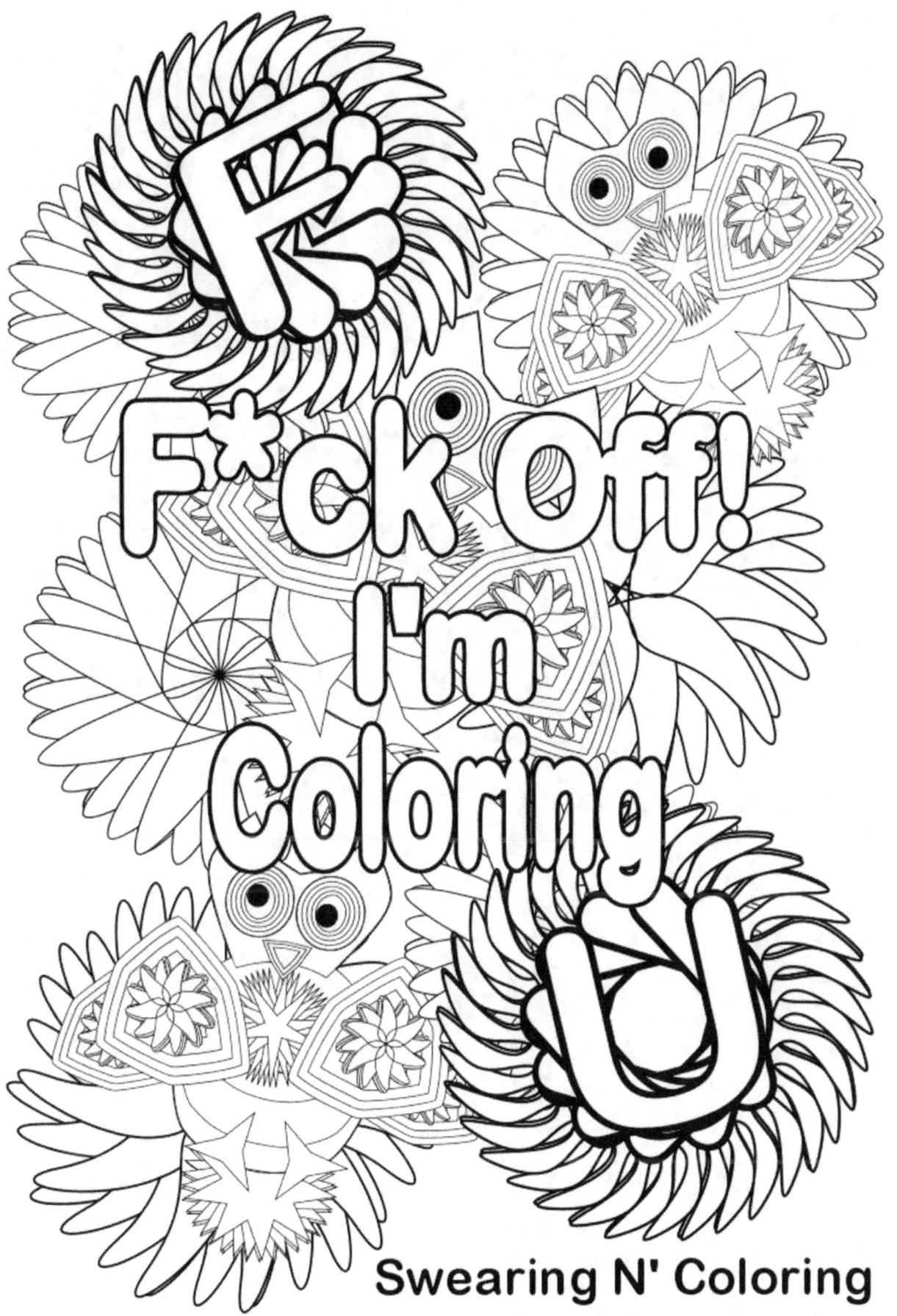

F*ck Off! I'm Coloring

Swearing N' Coloring

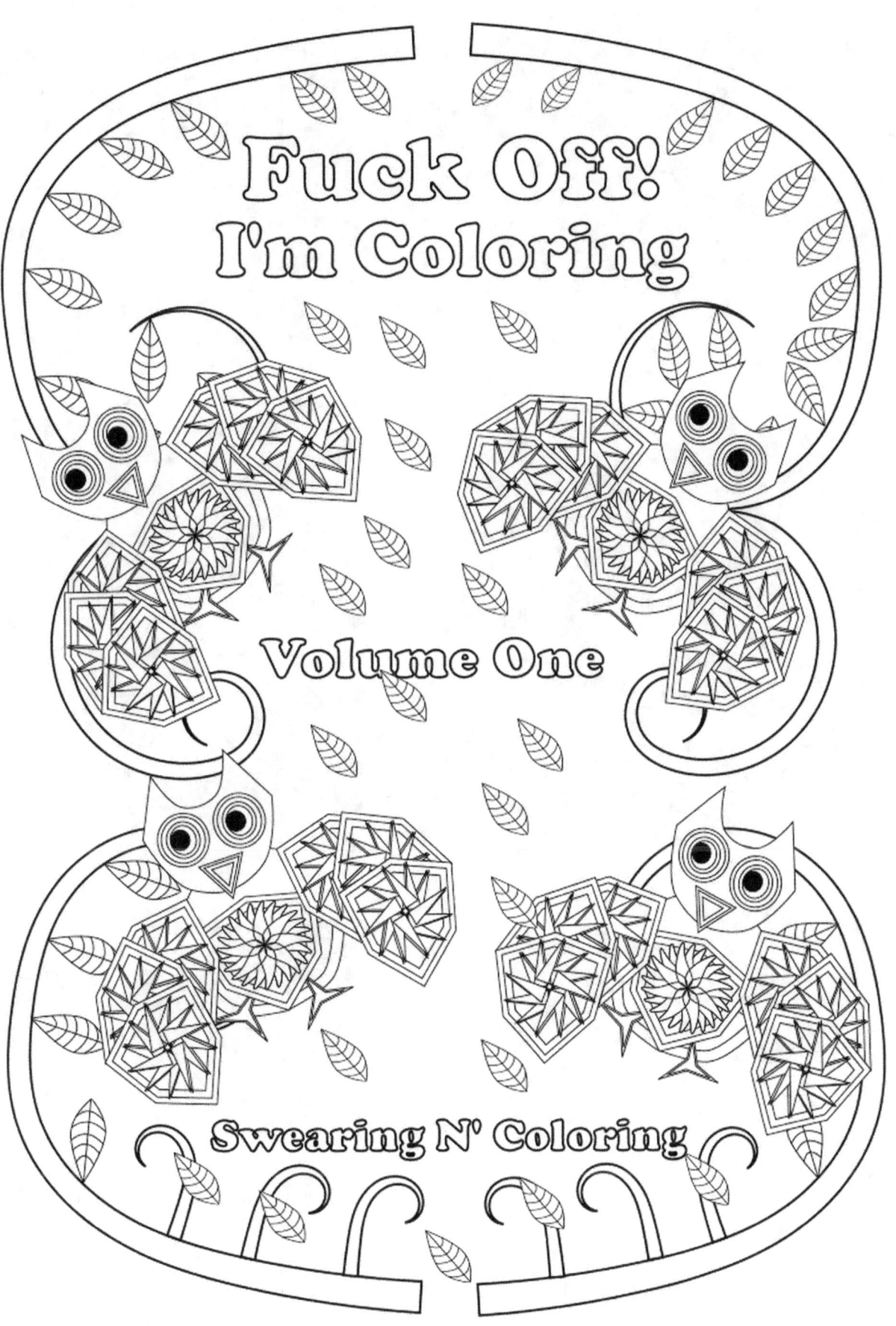

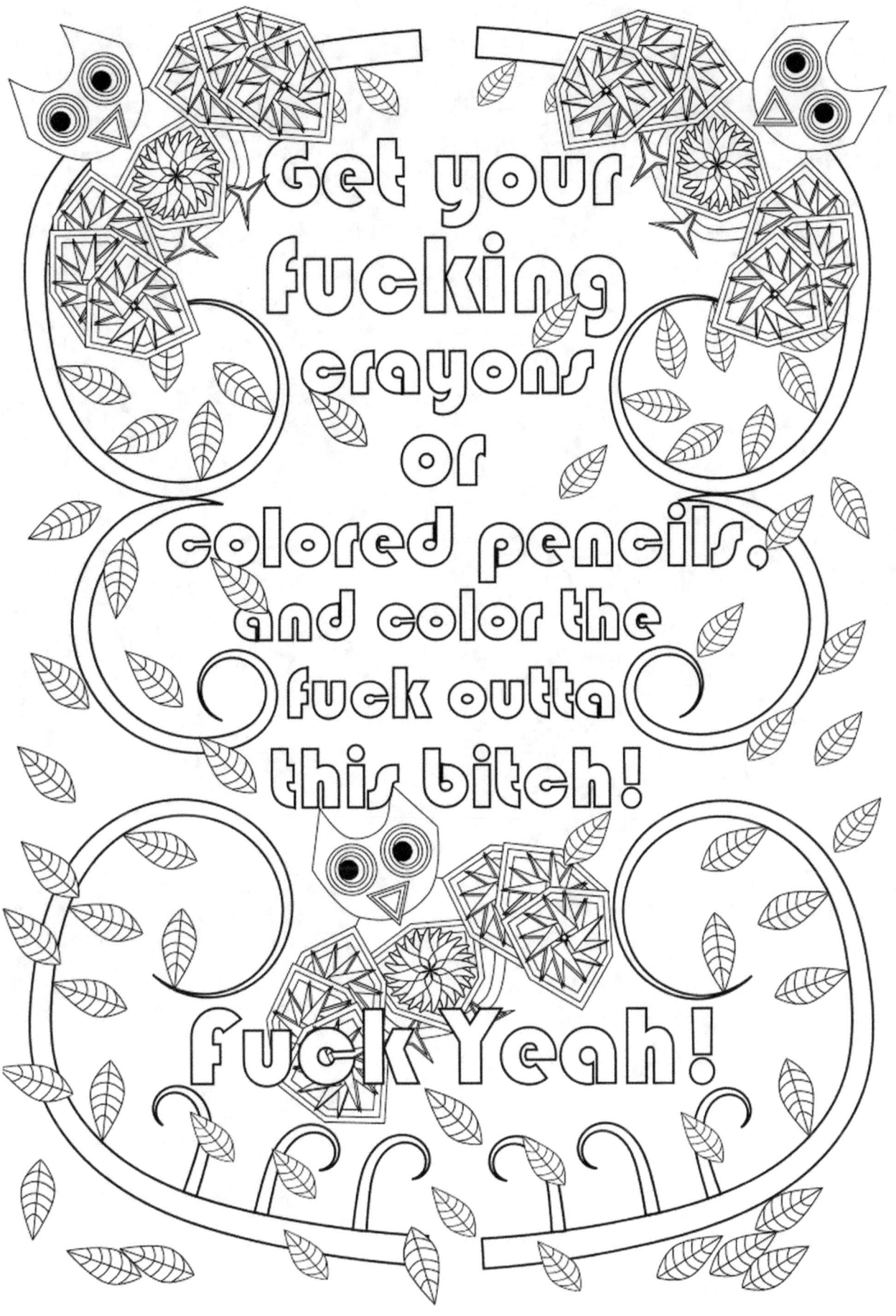

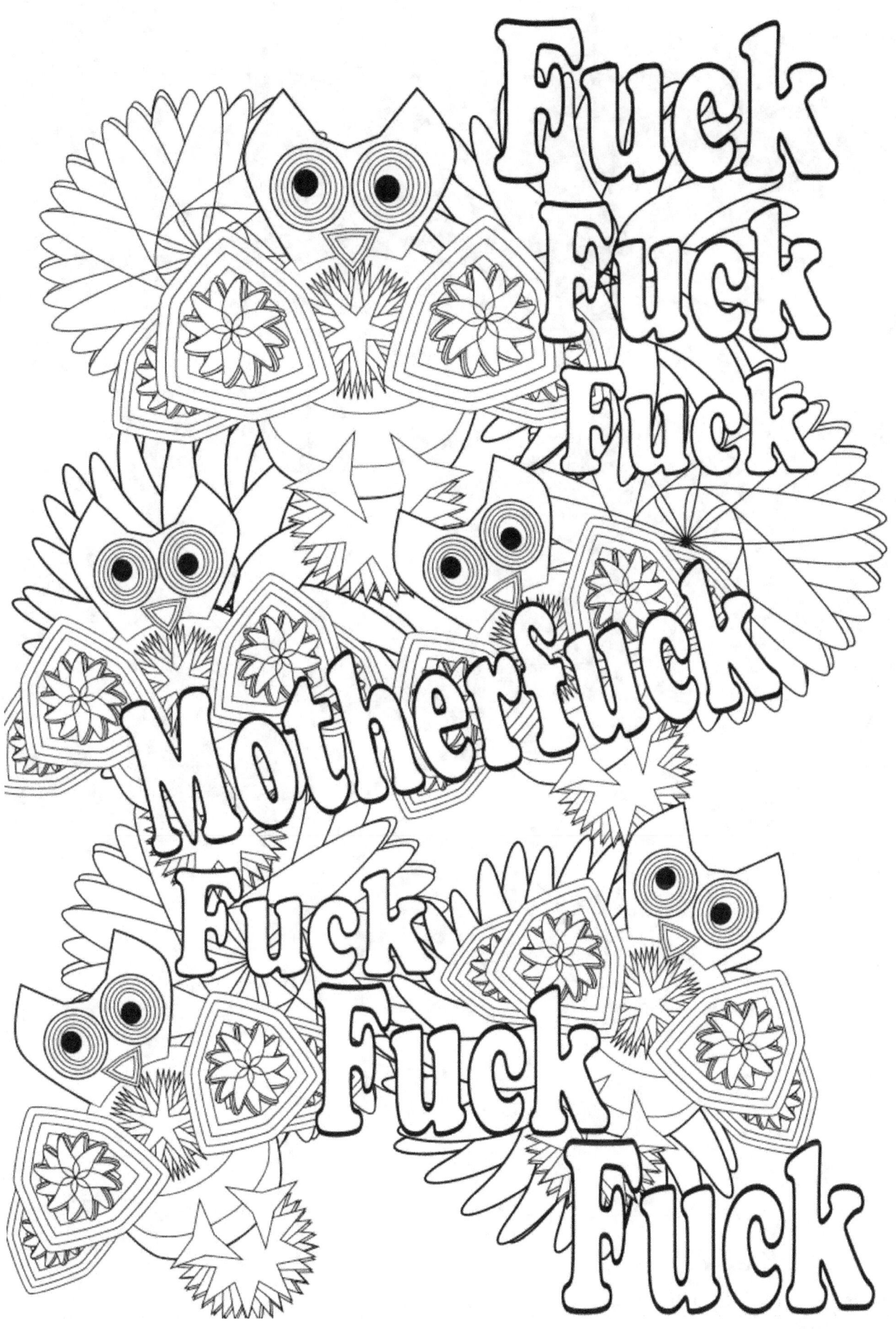

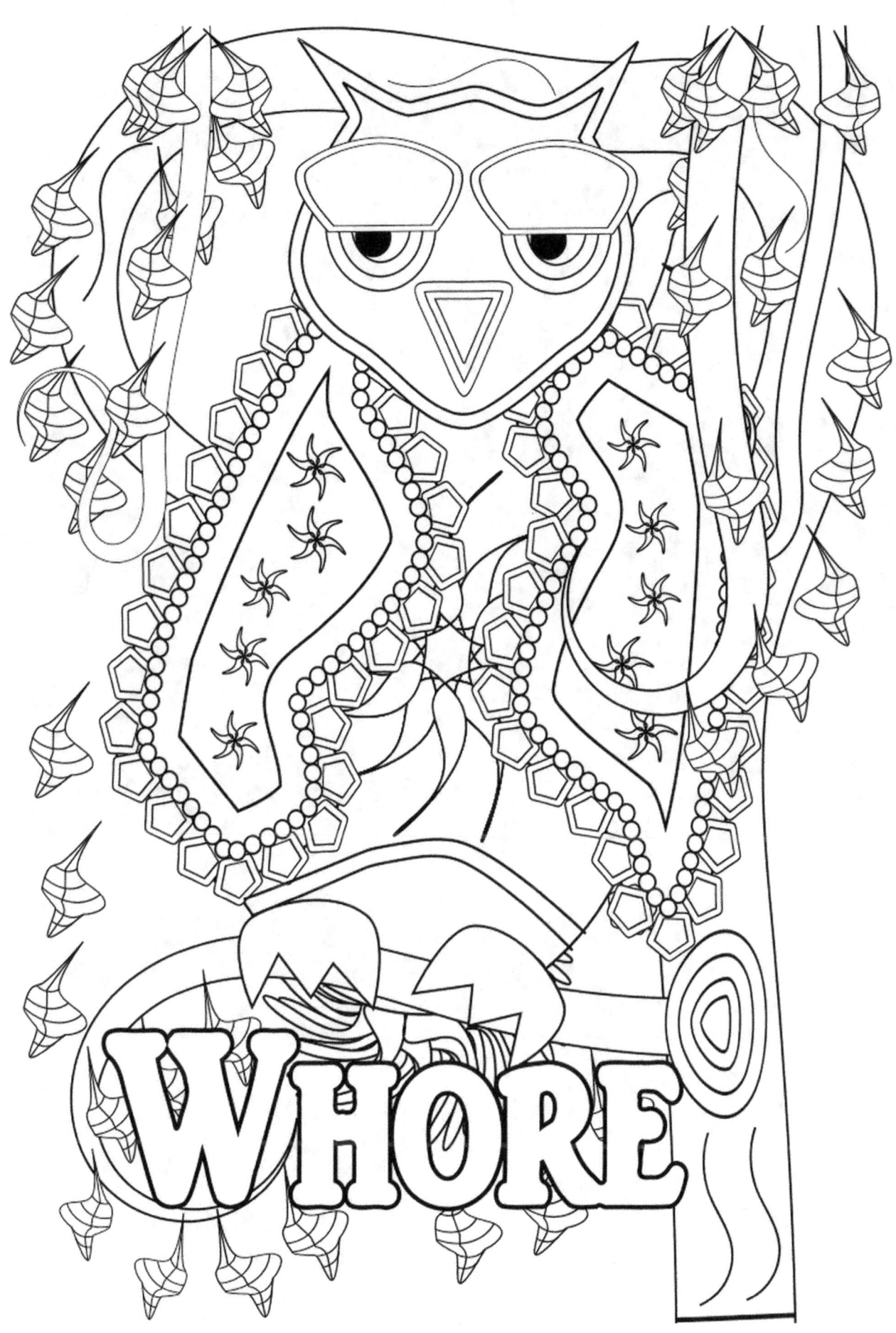

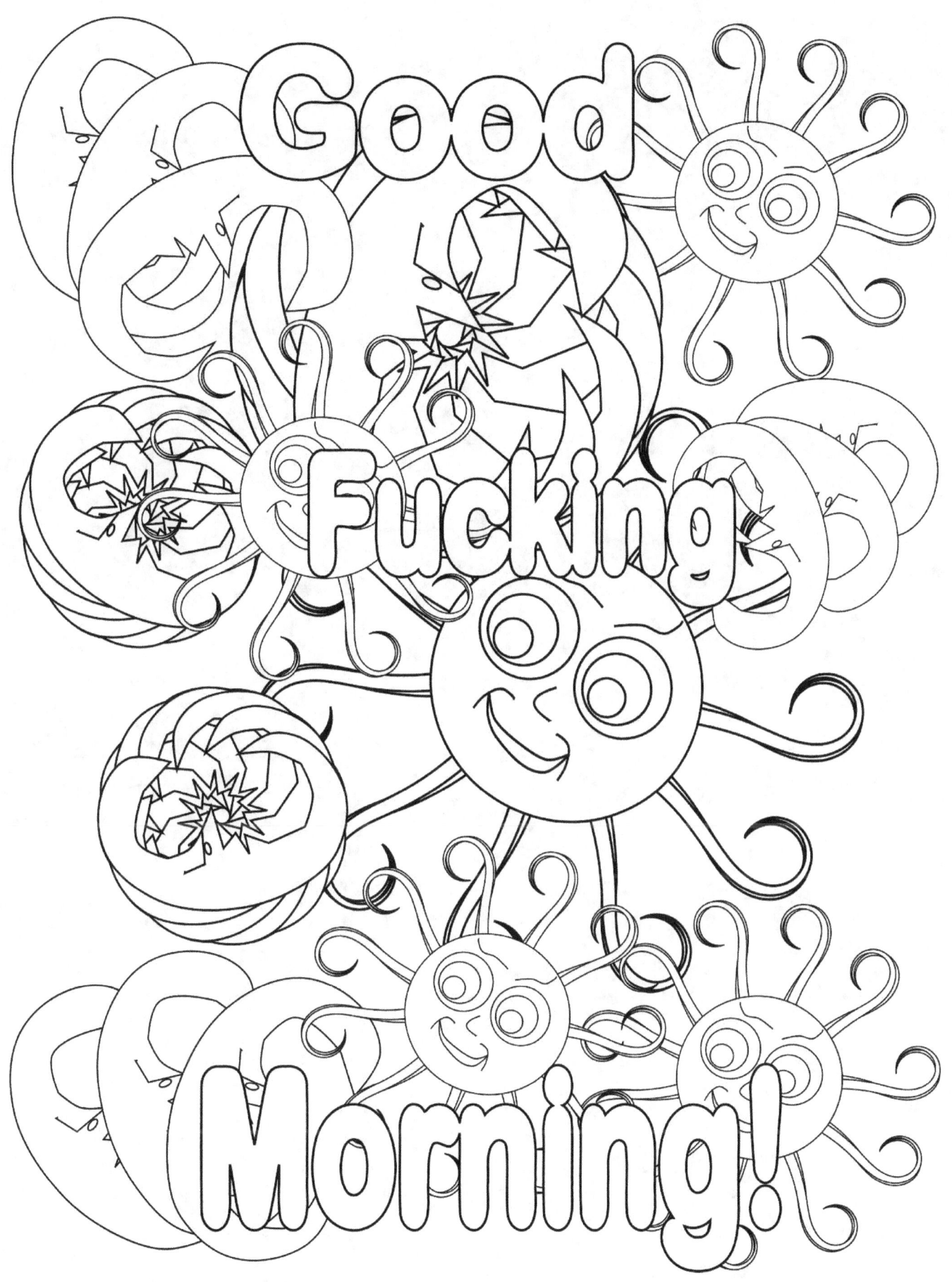

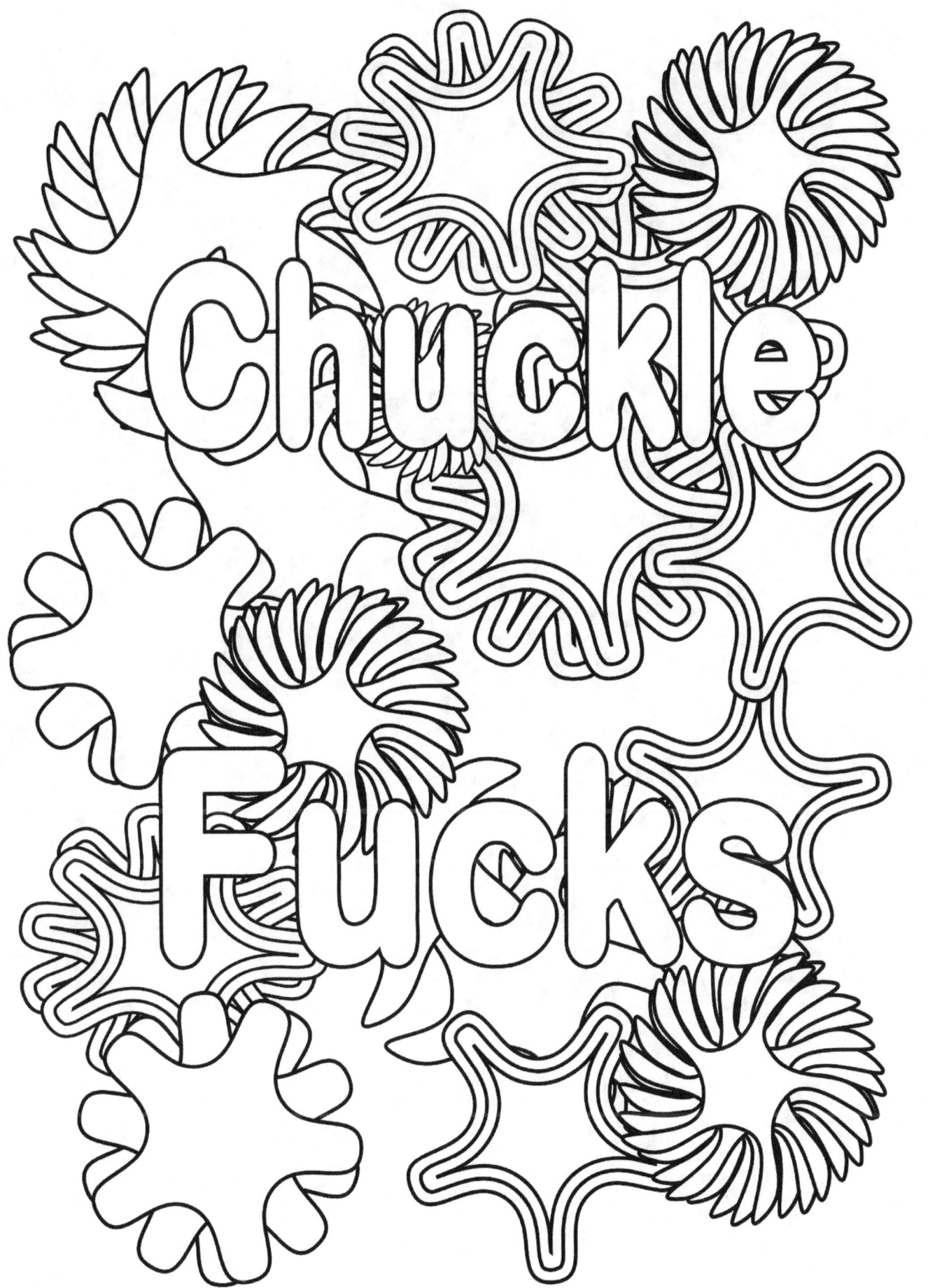

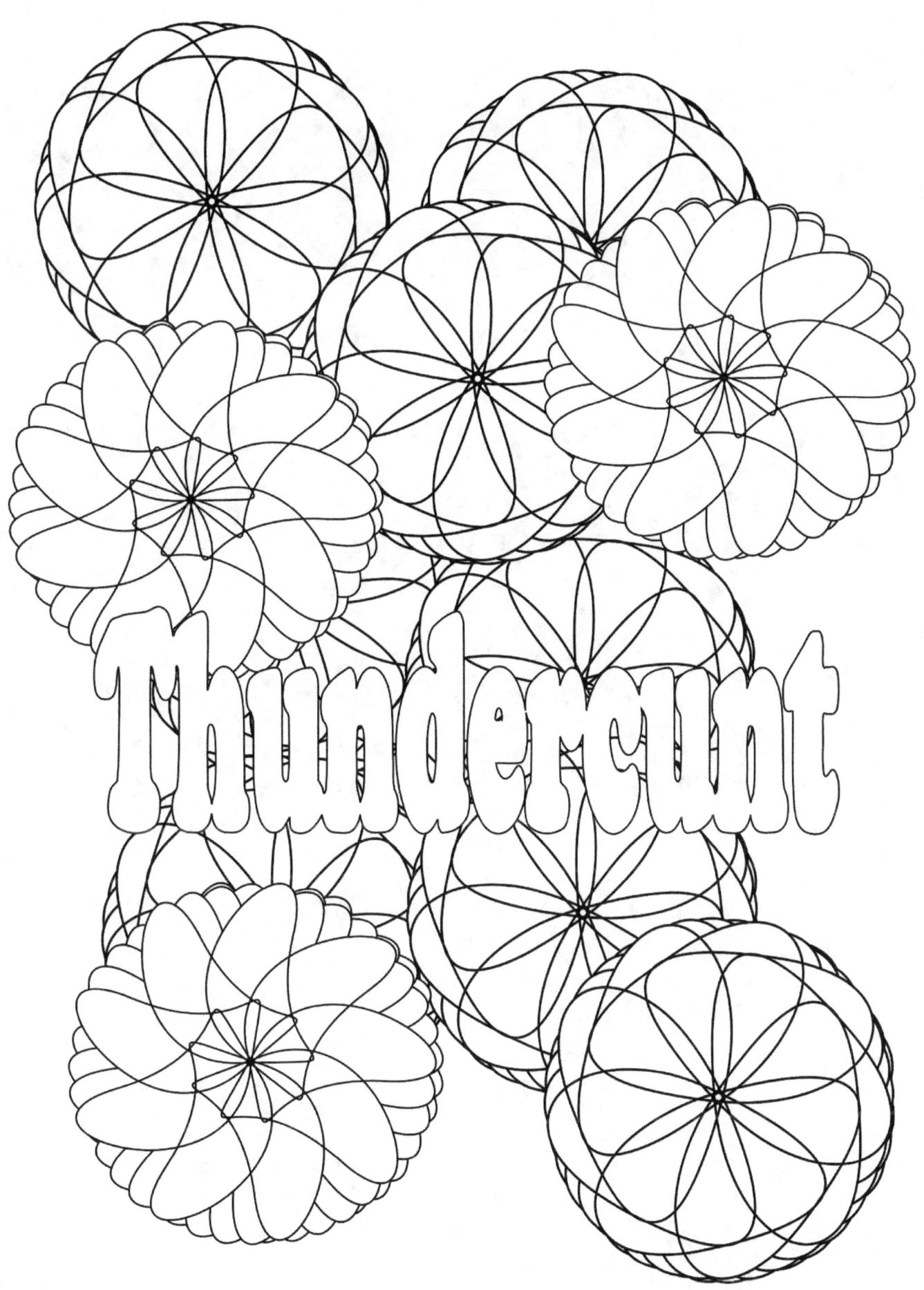

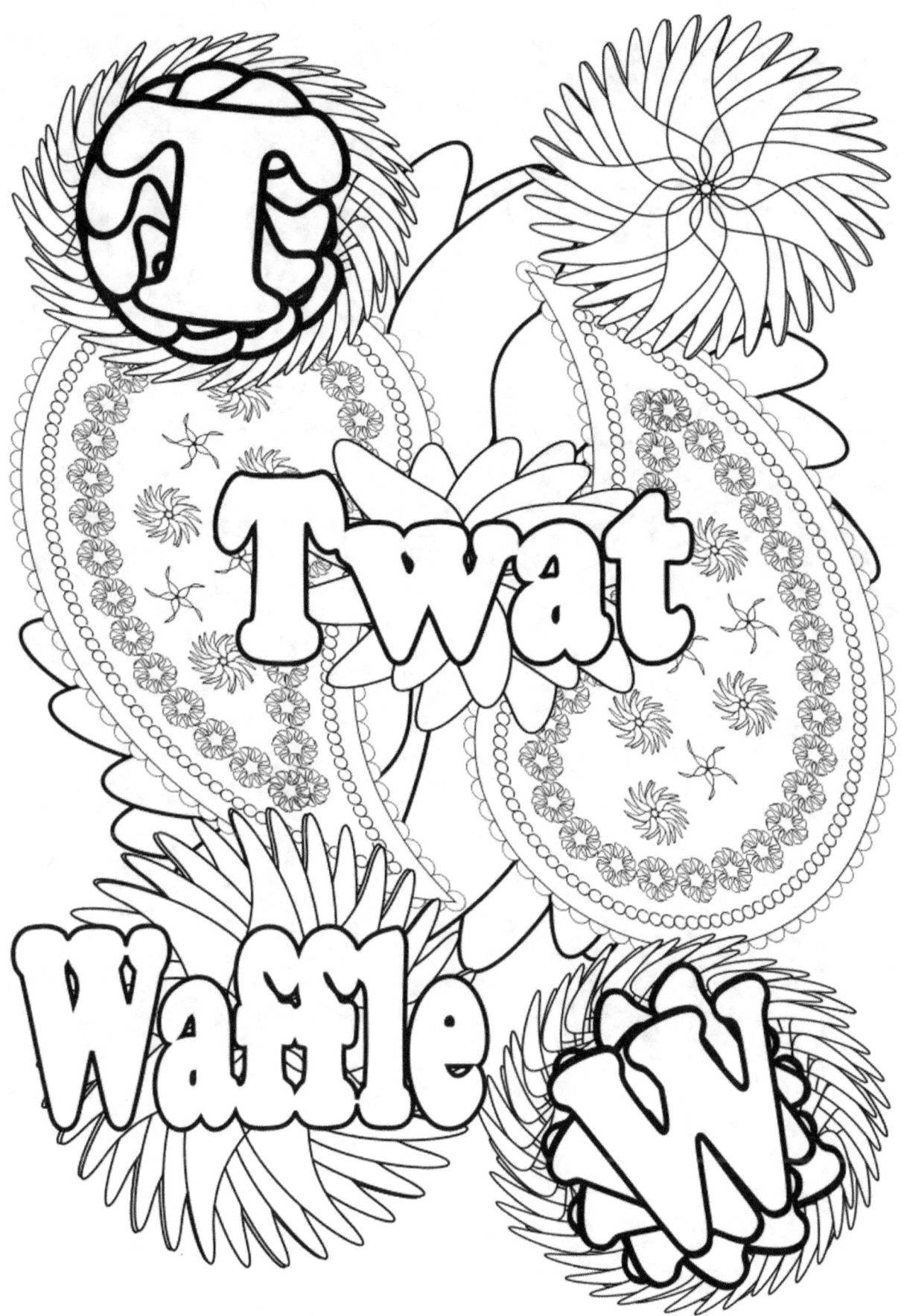

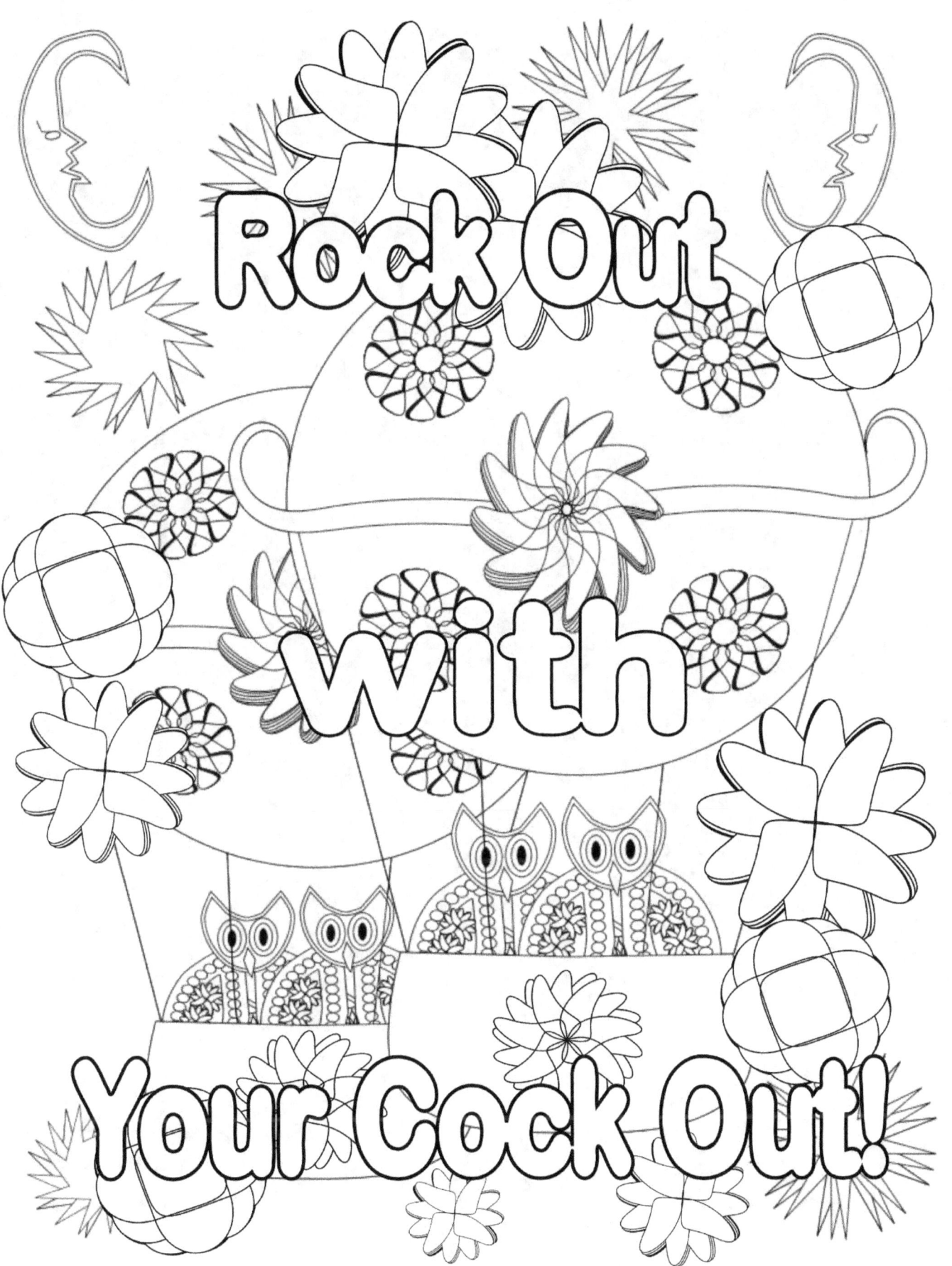

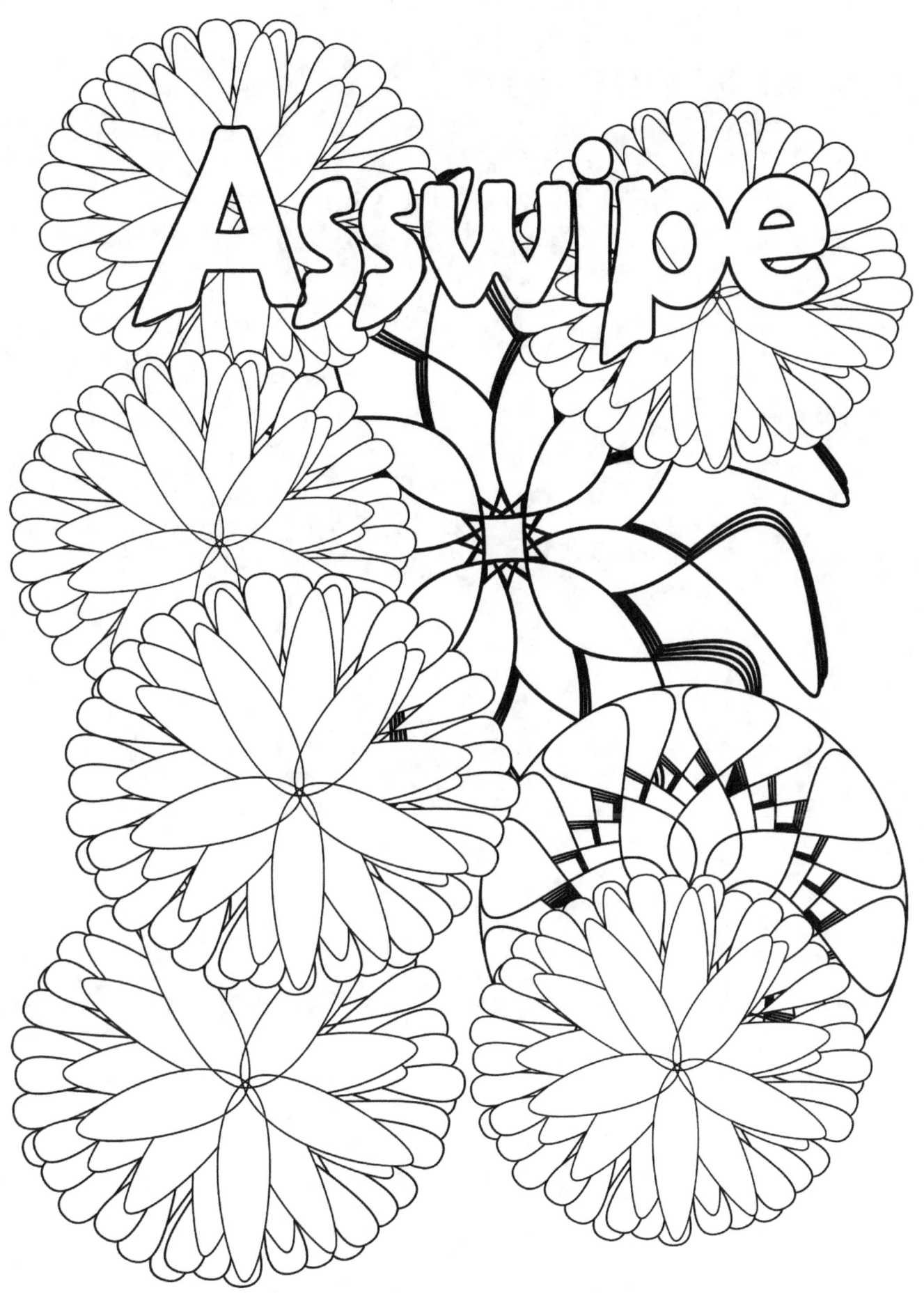

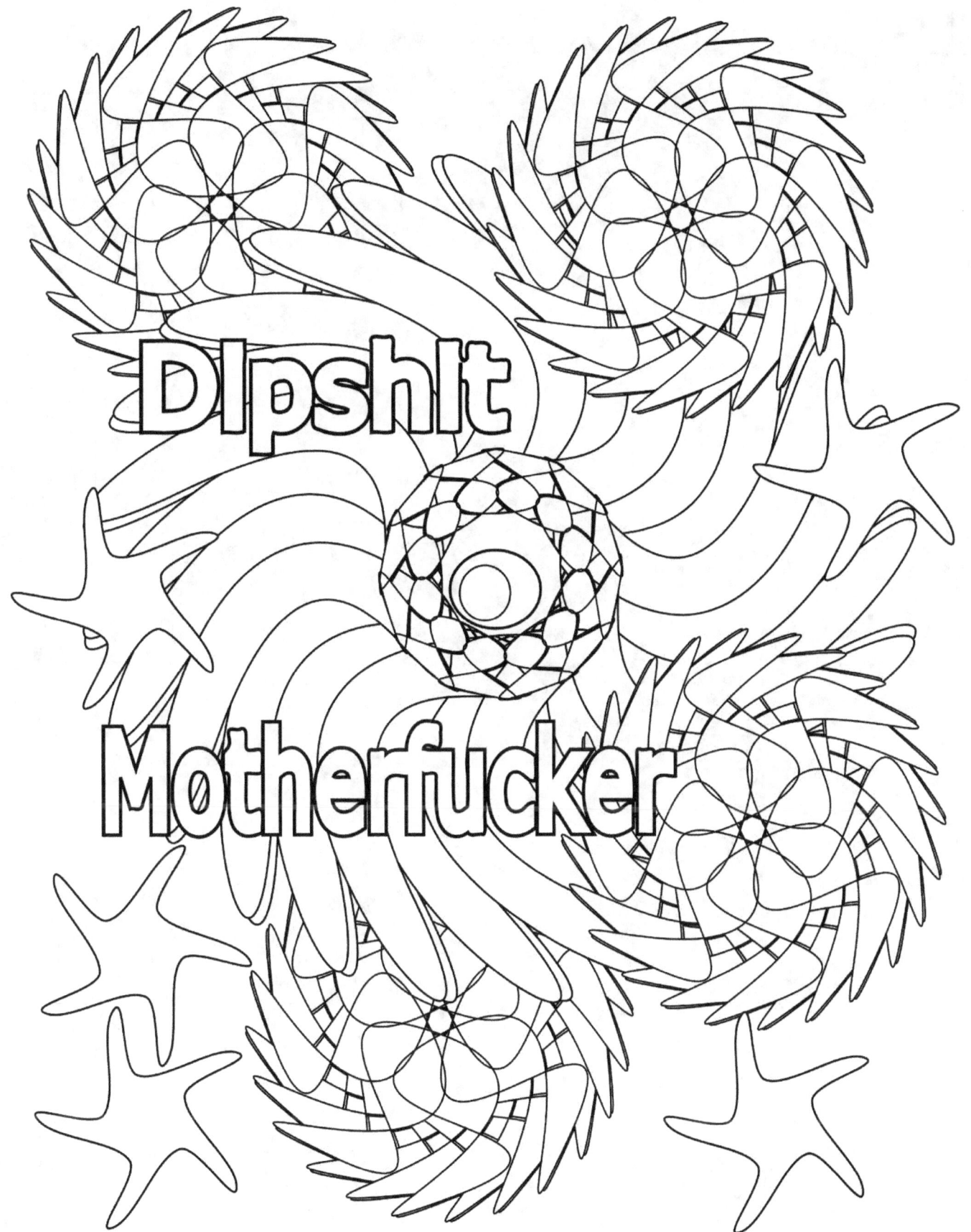

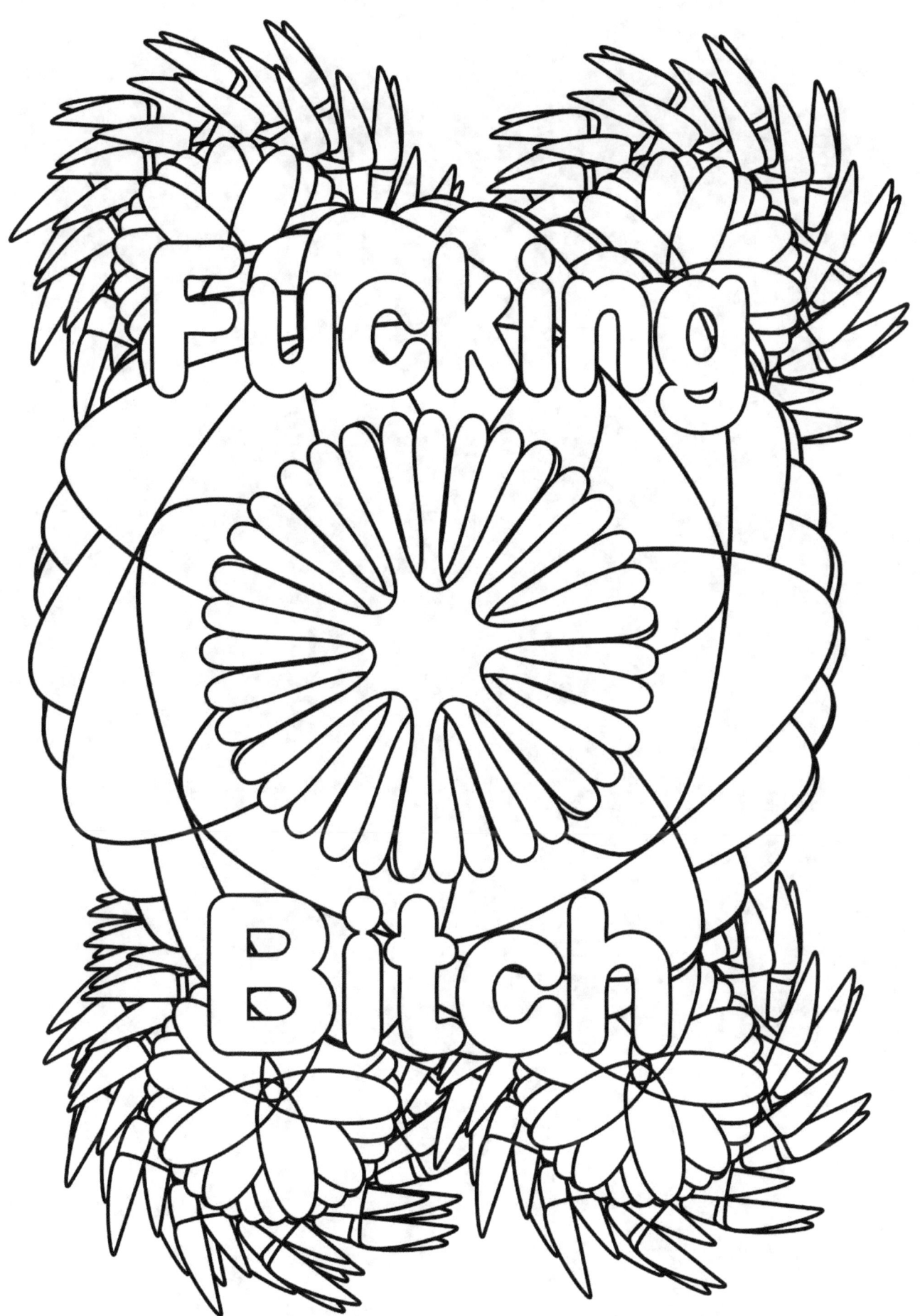

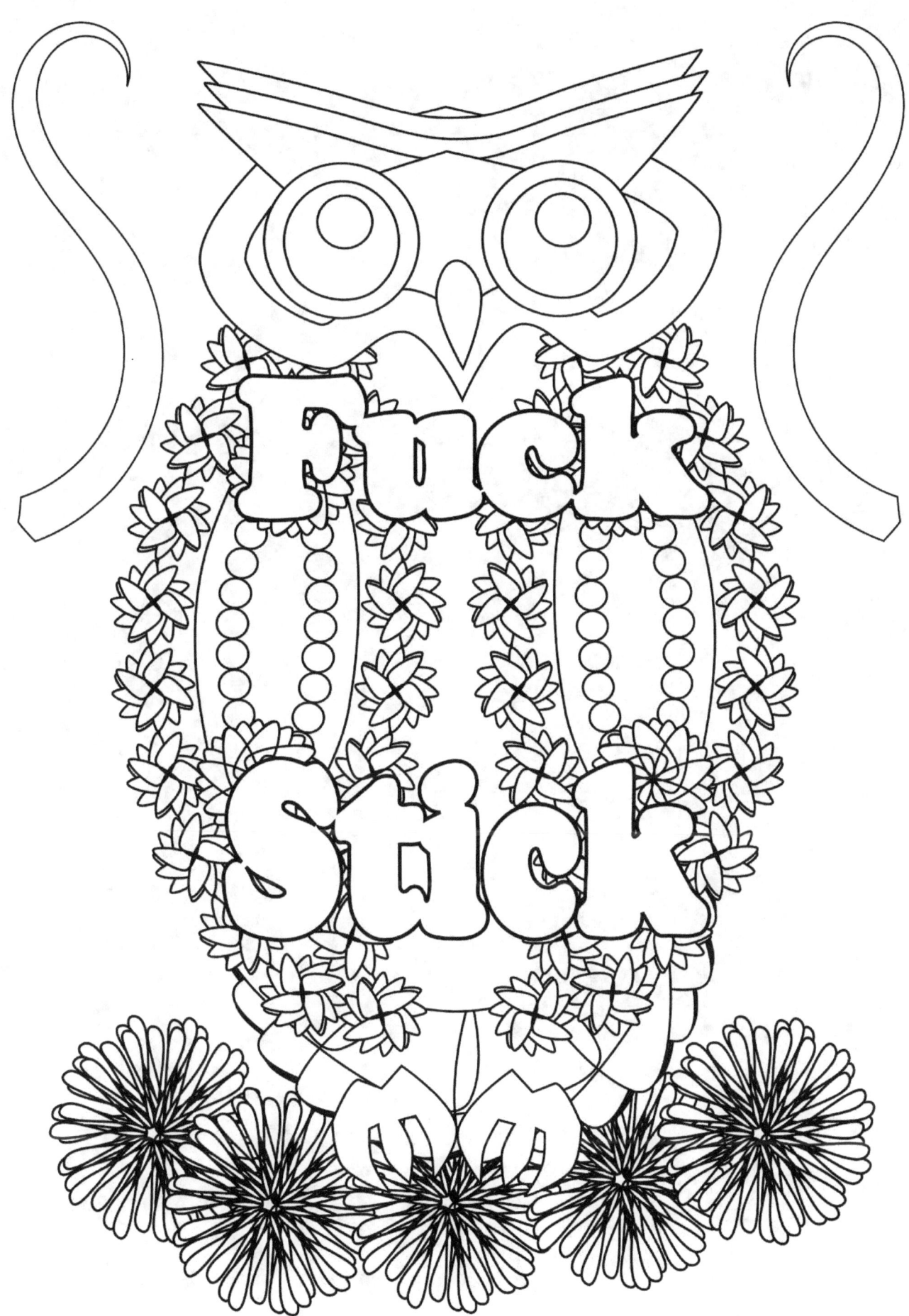

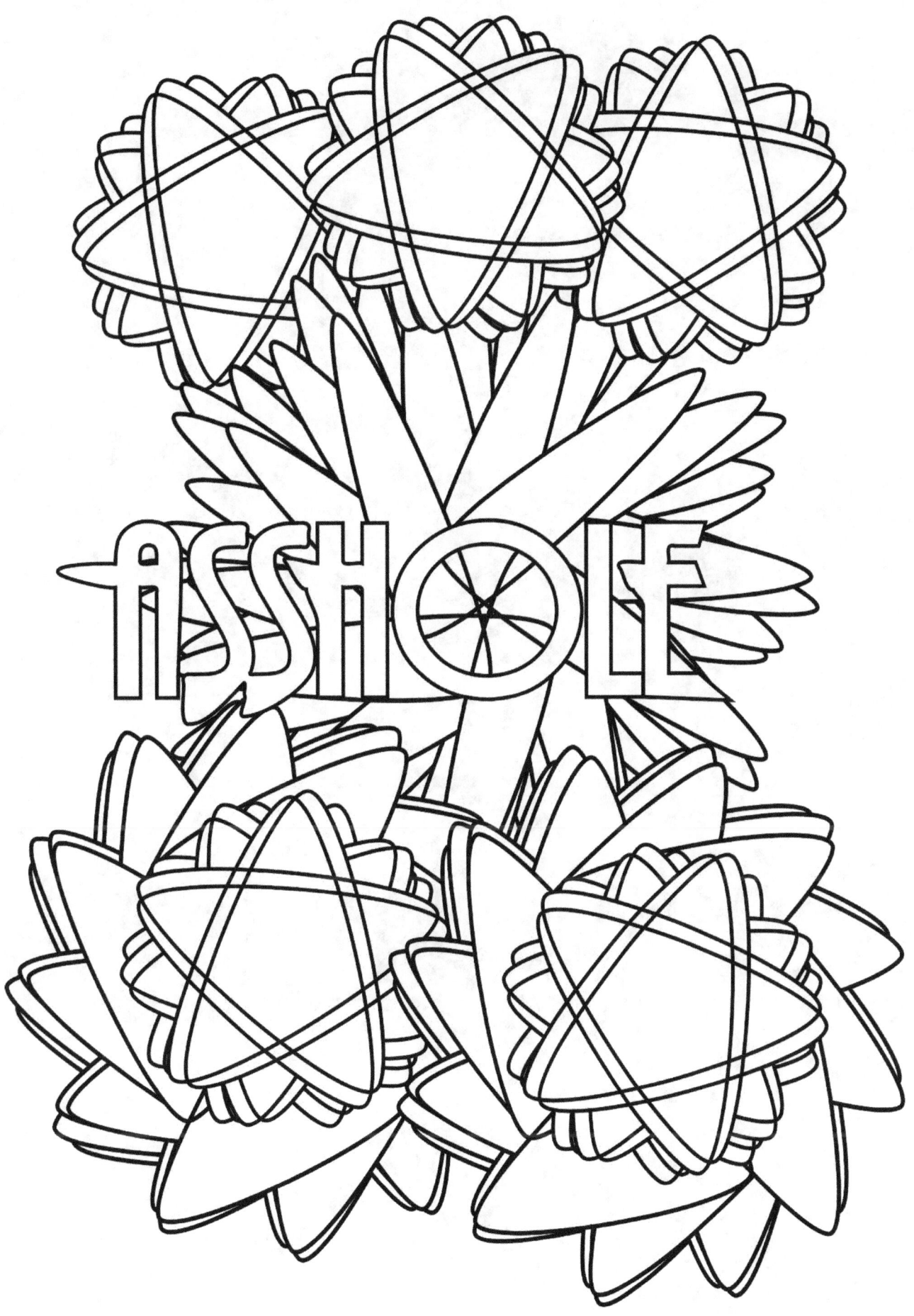

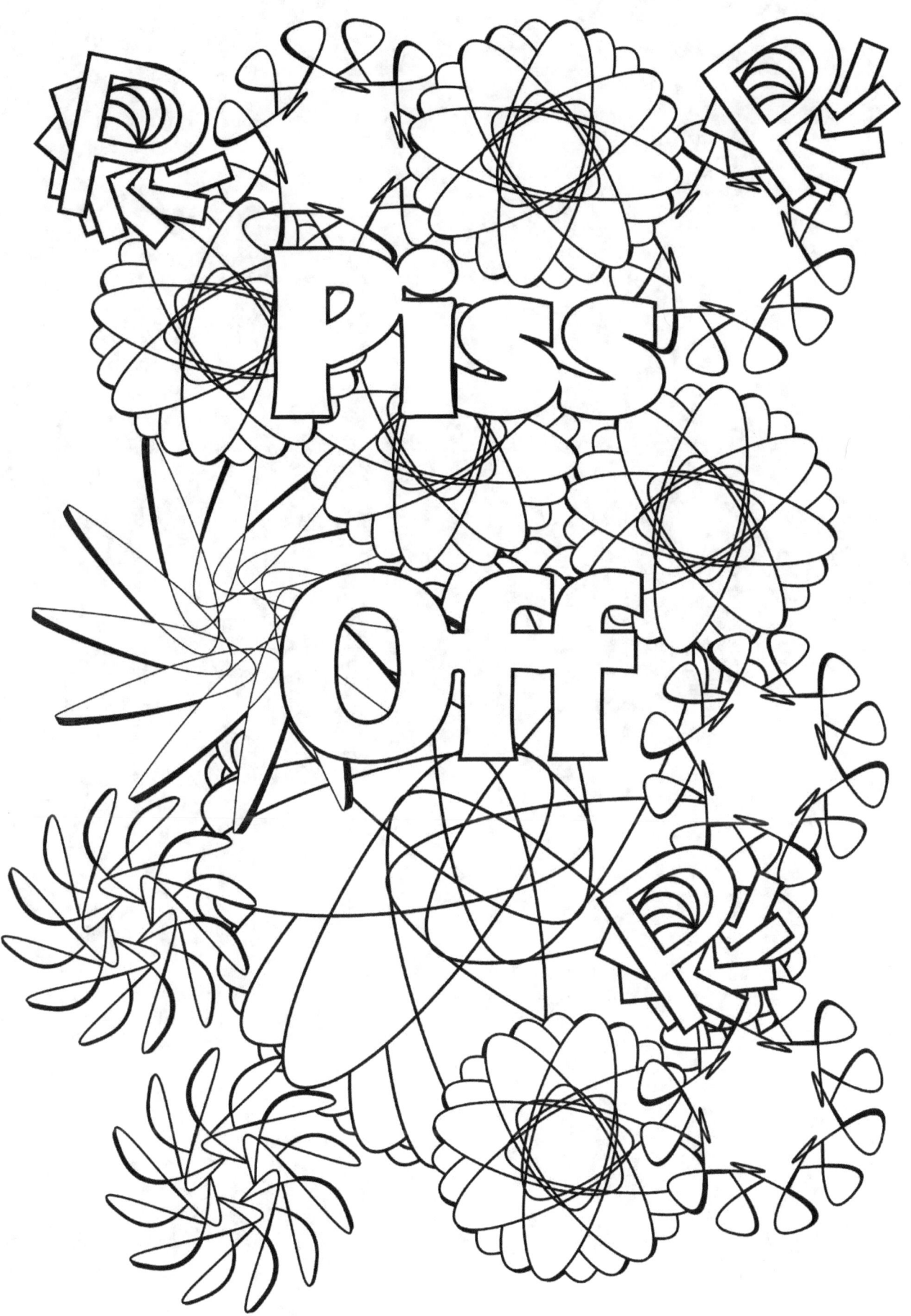

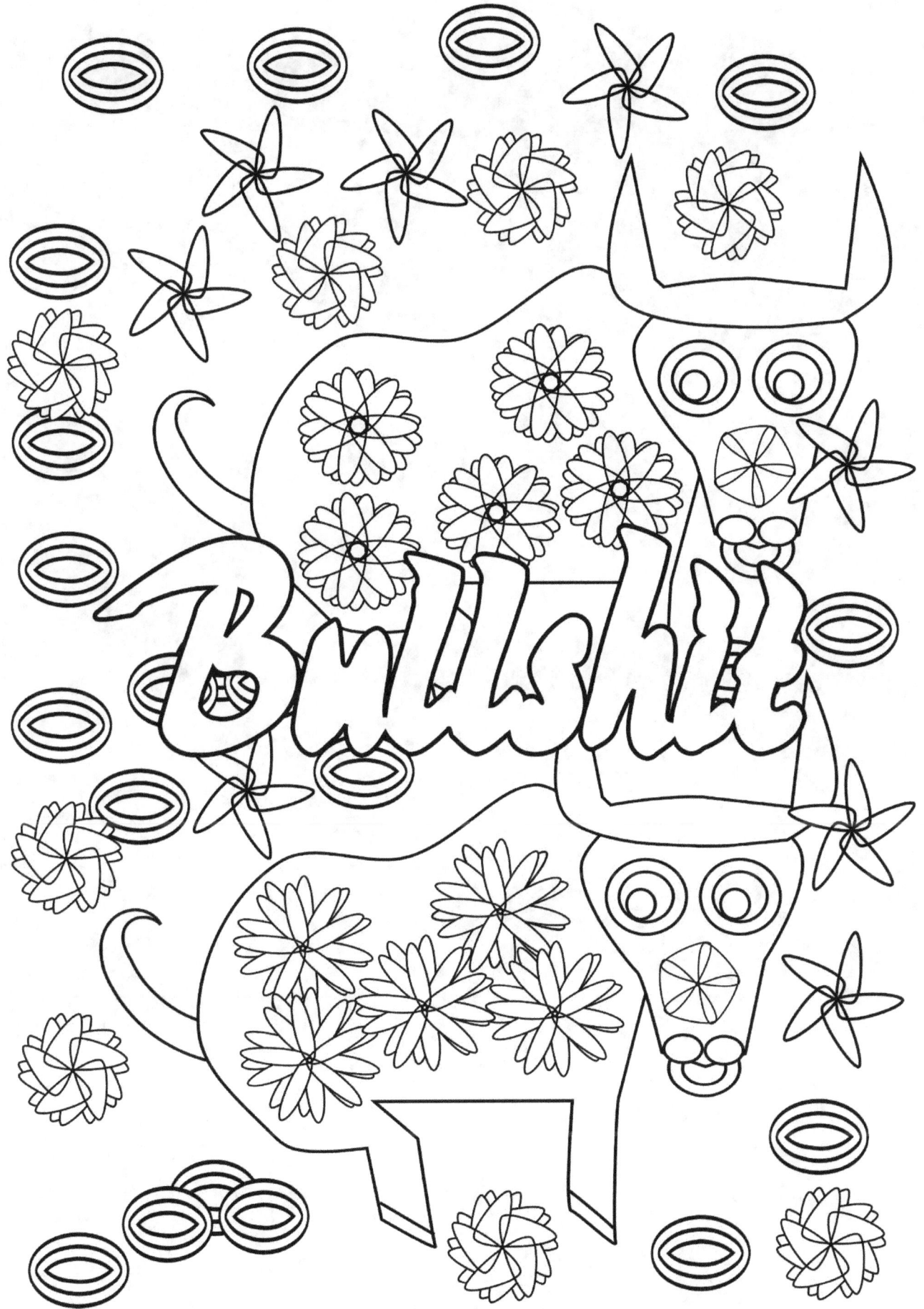

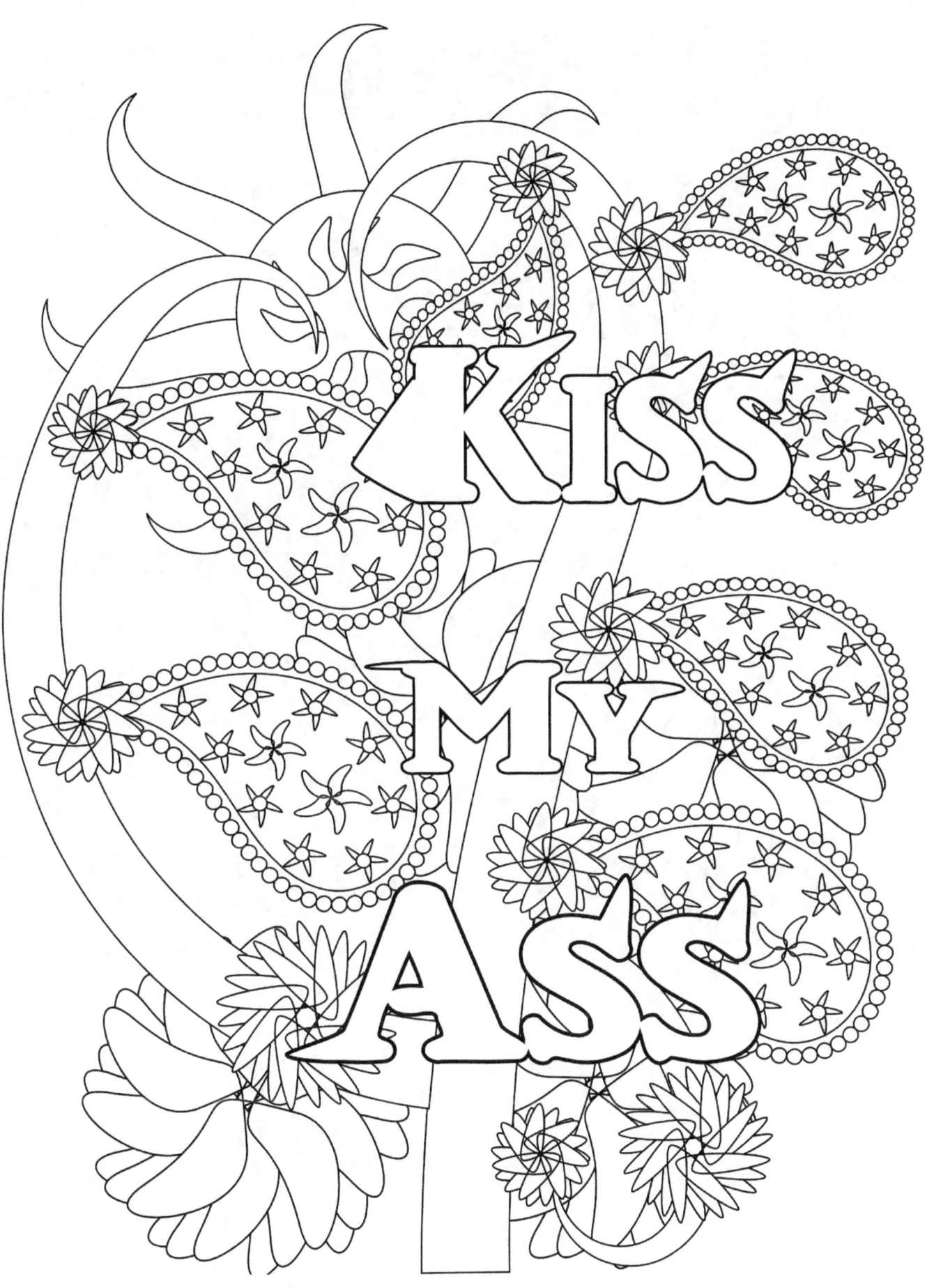

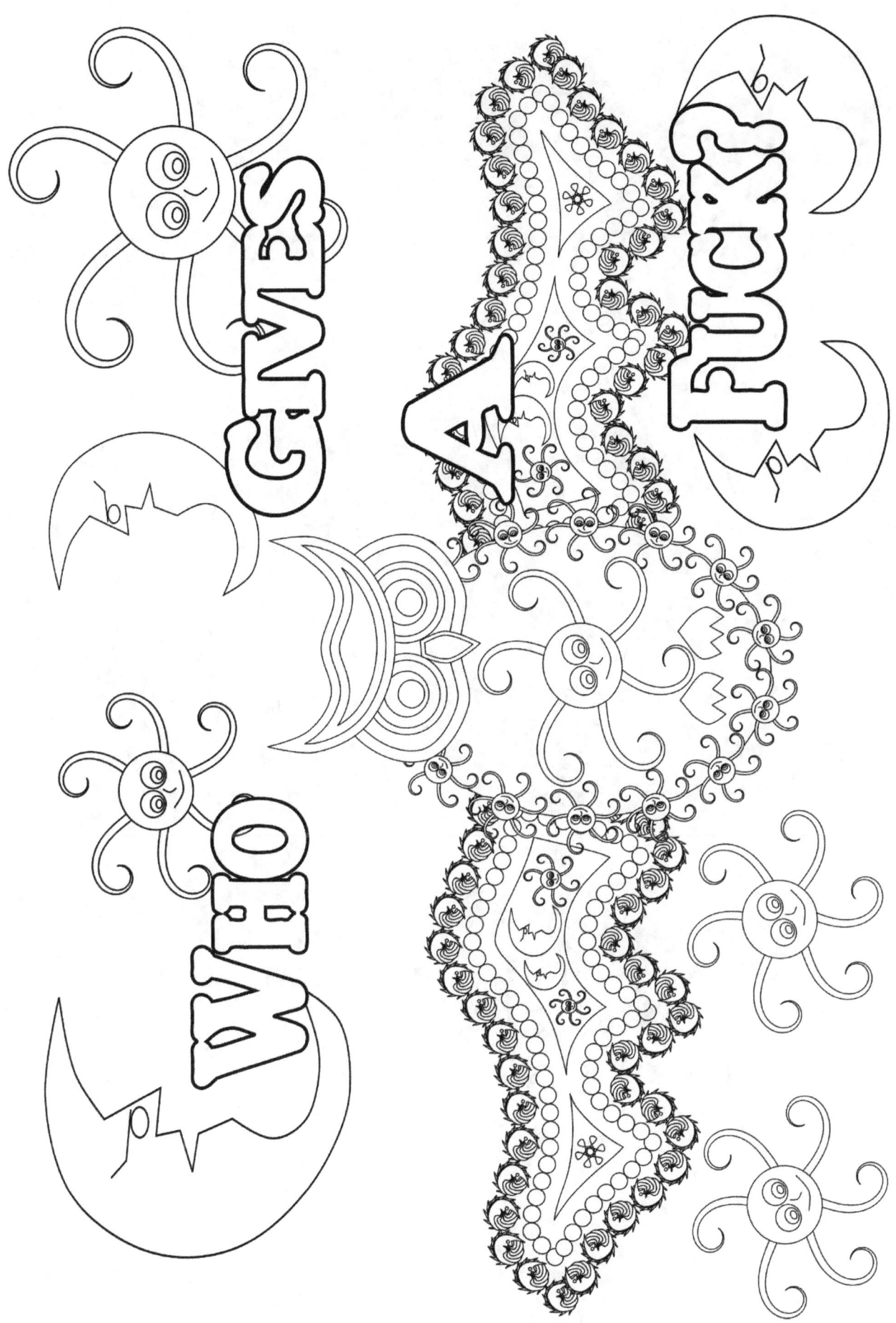

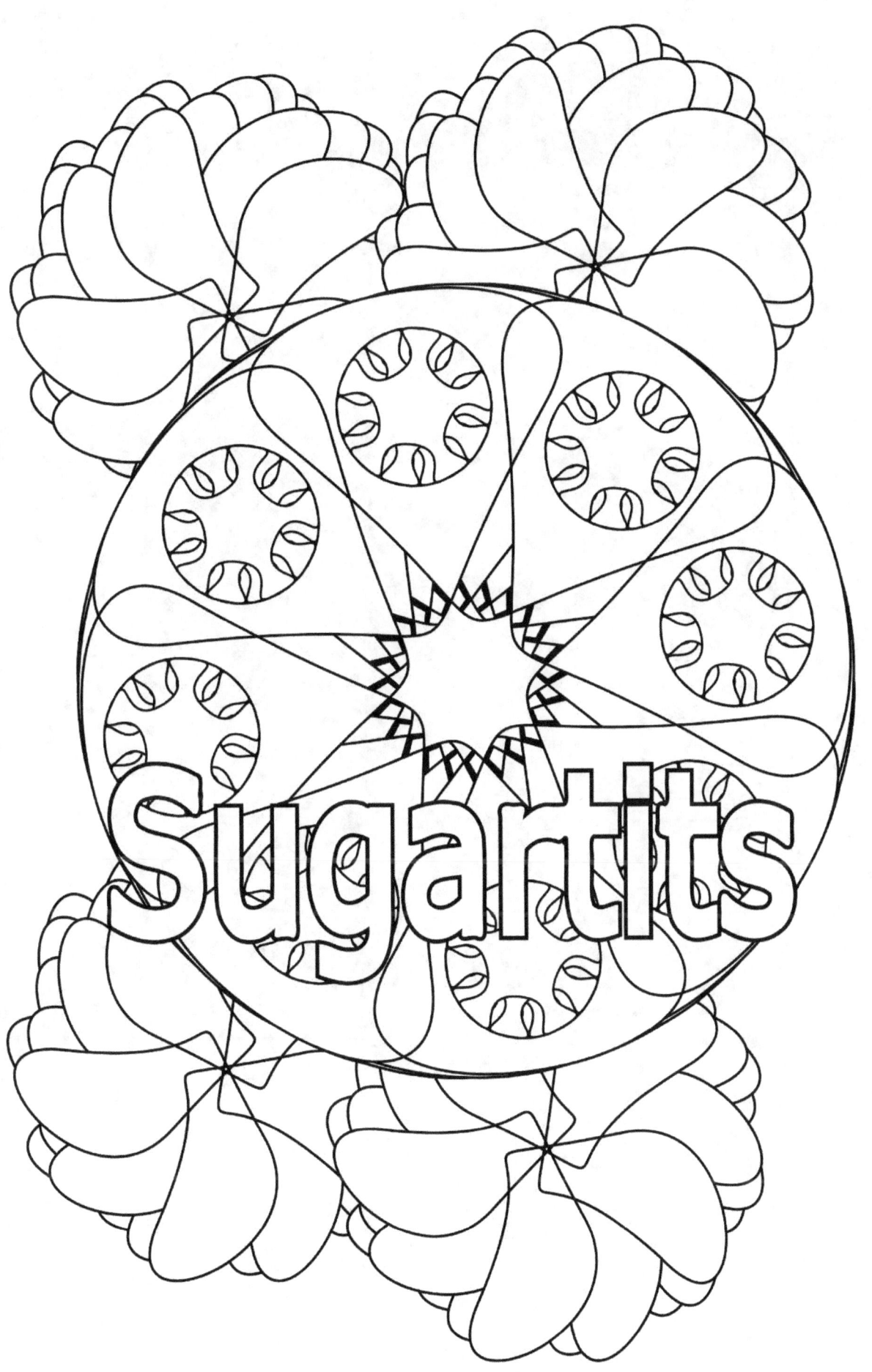

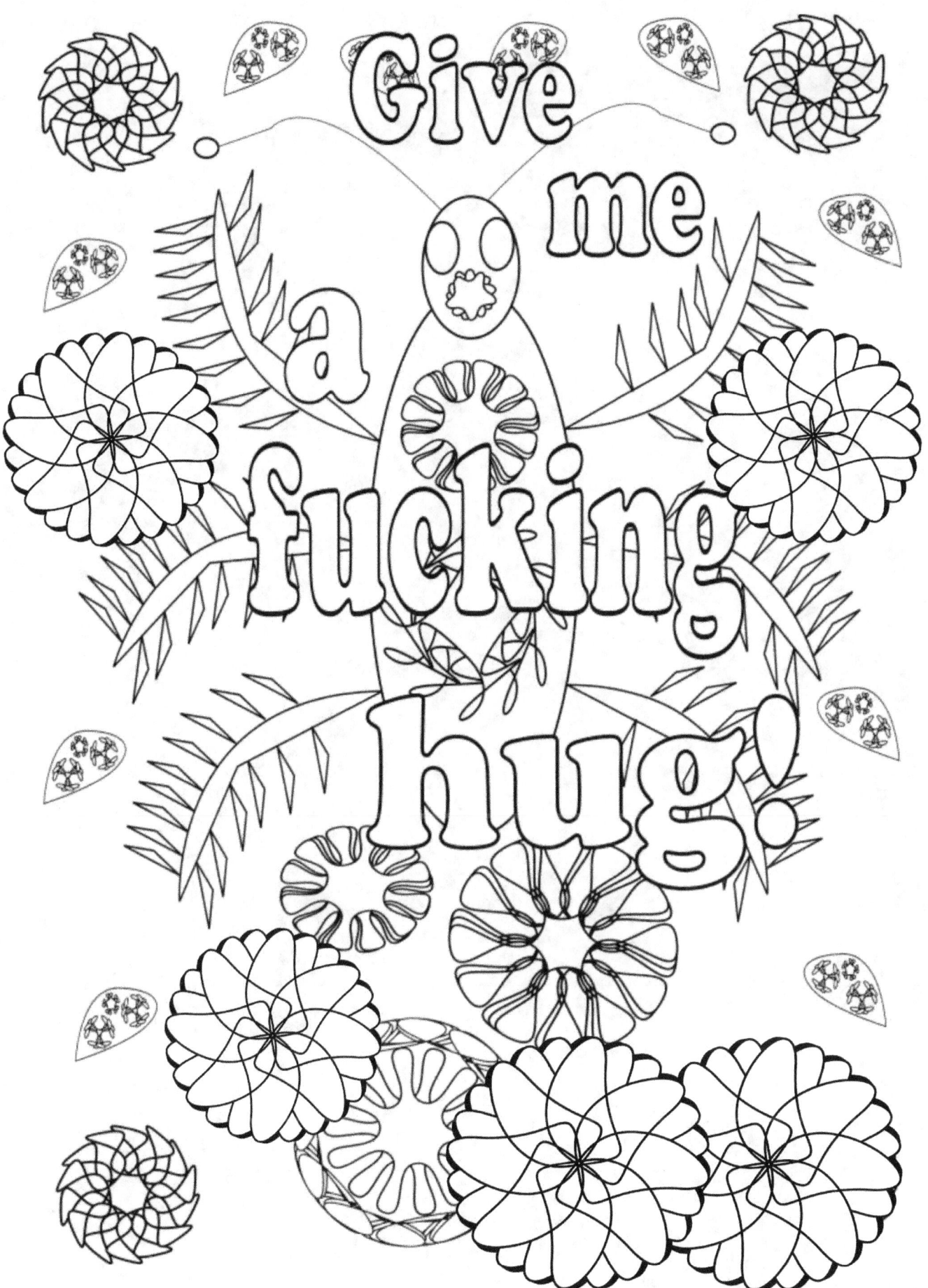

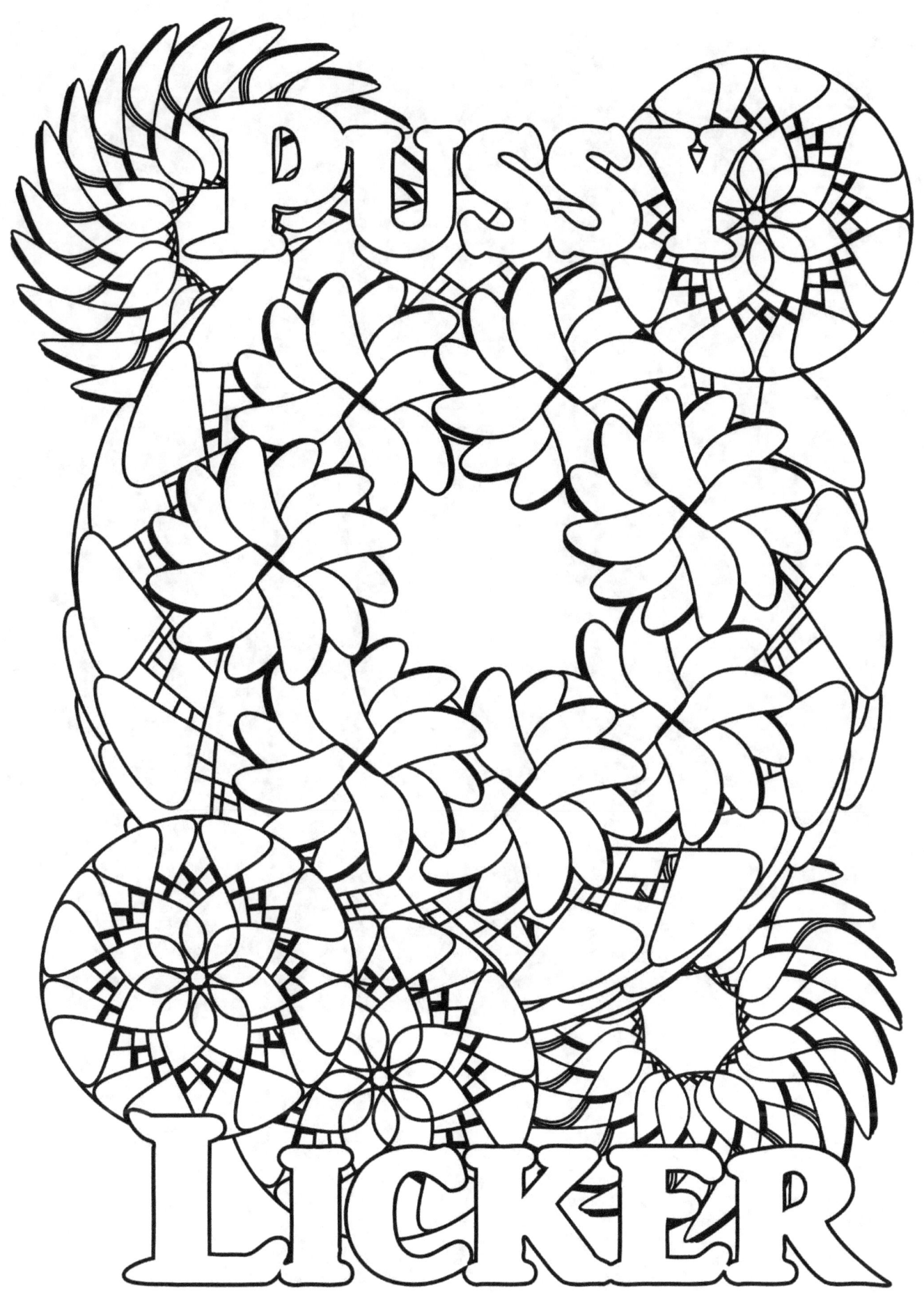

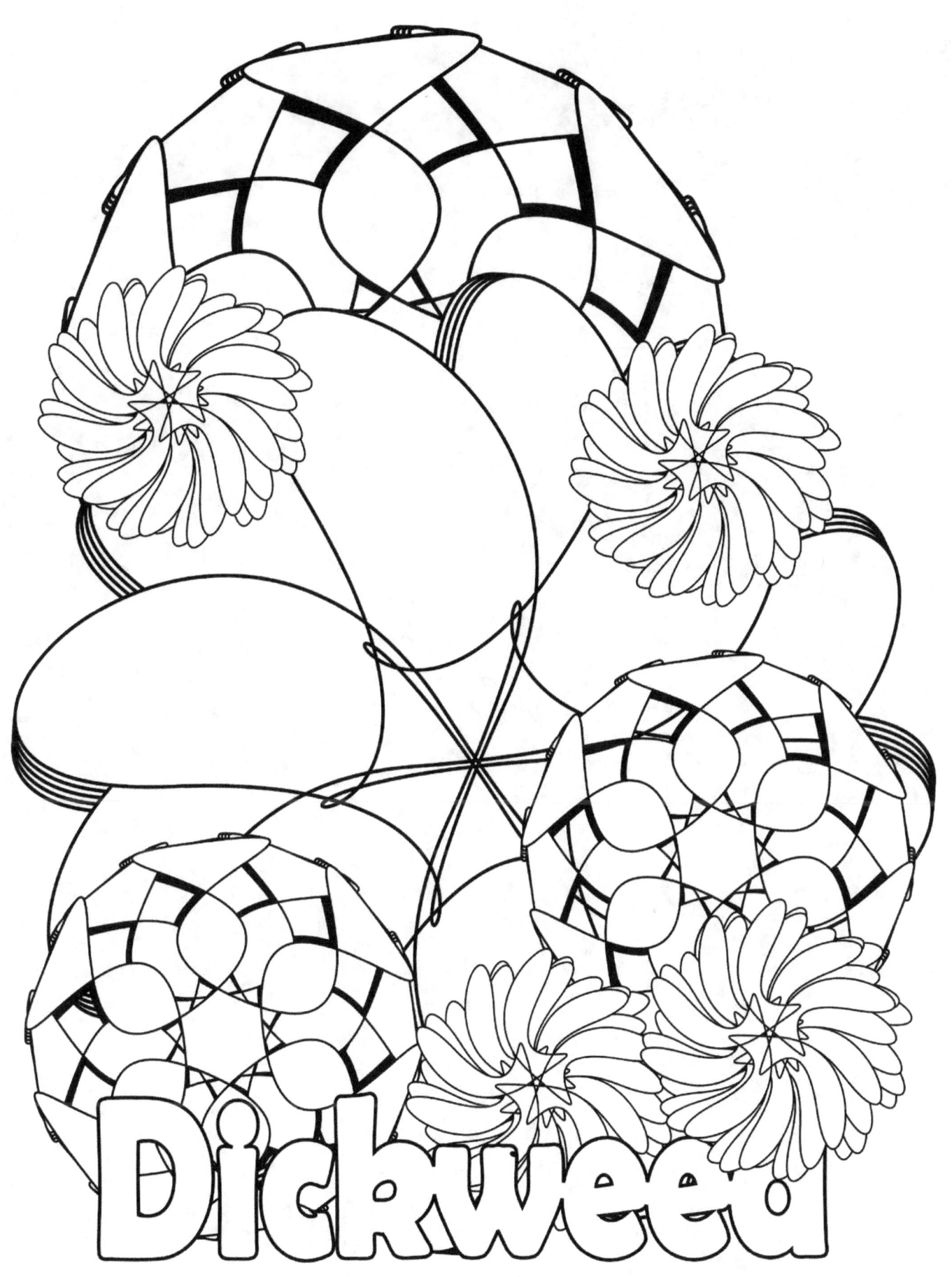

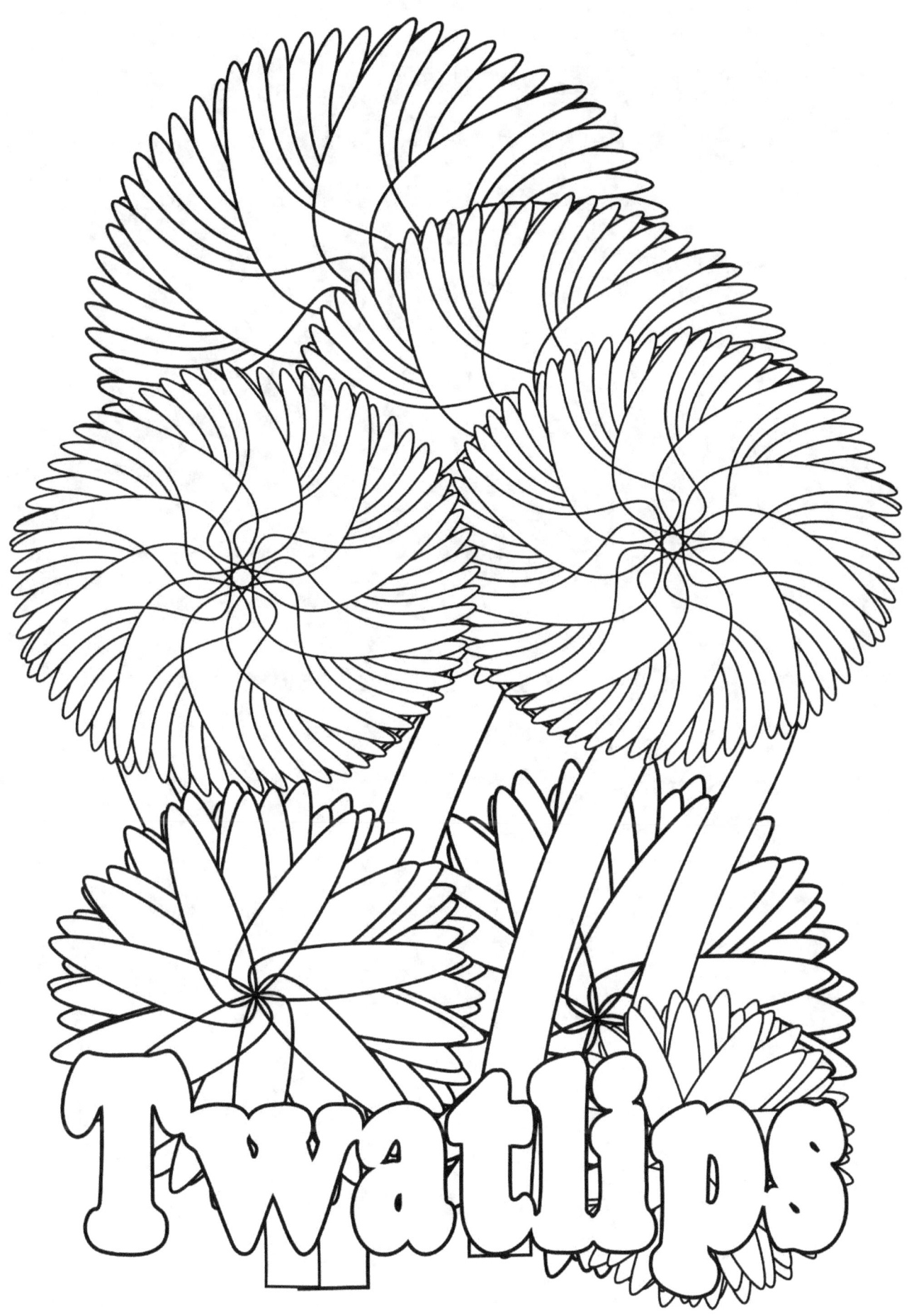

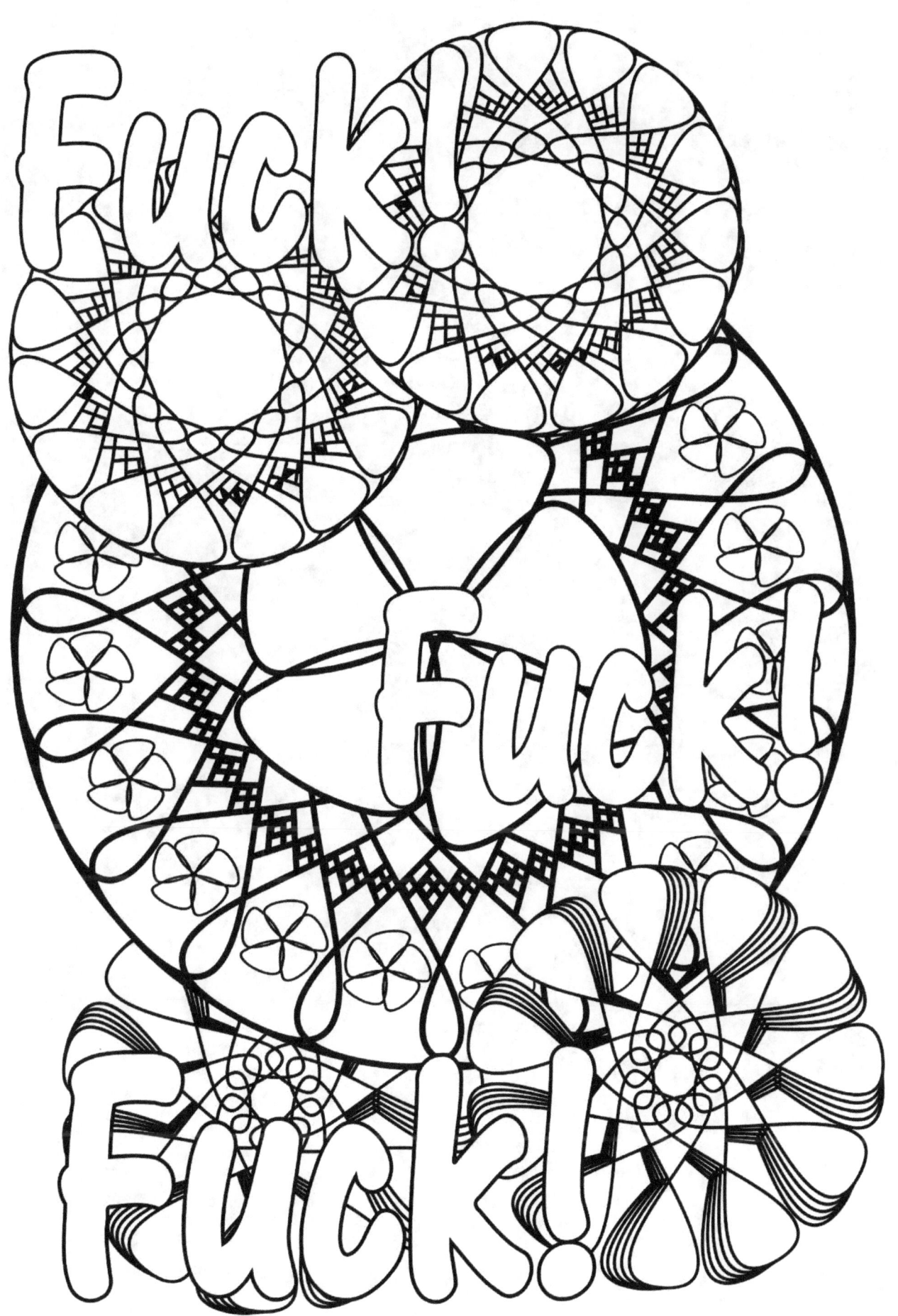

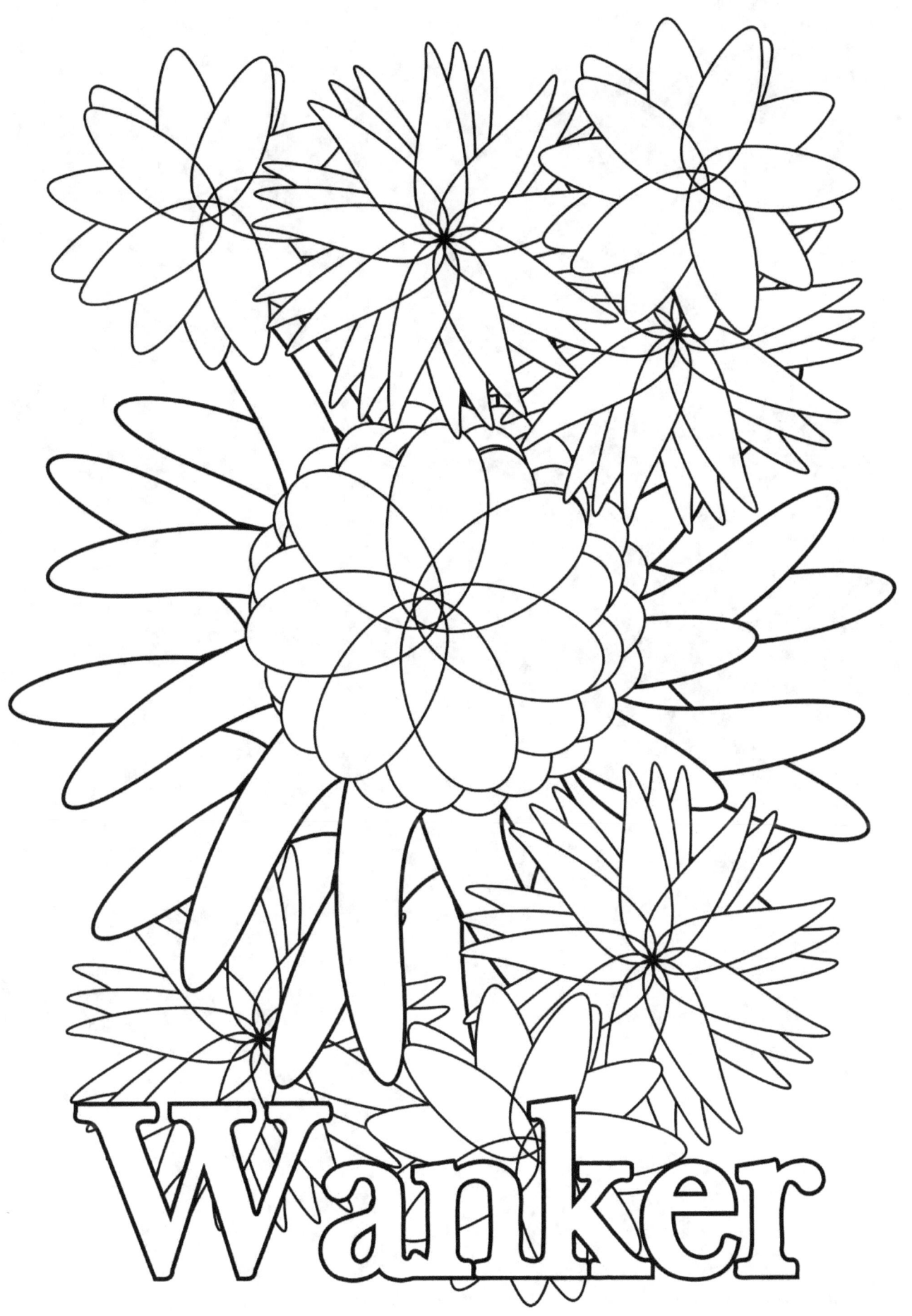

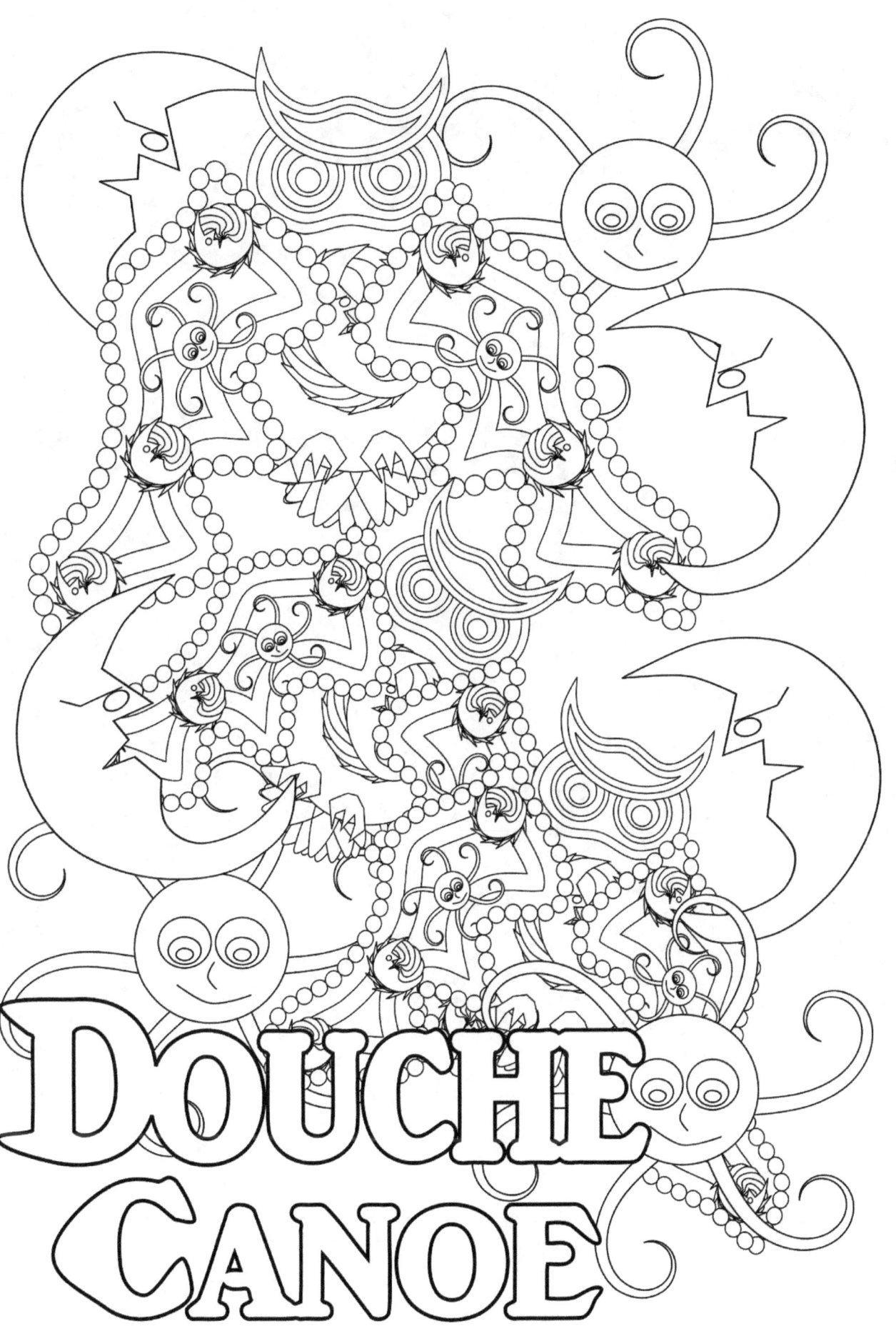

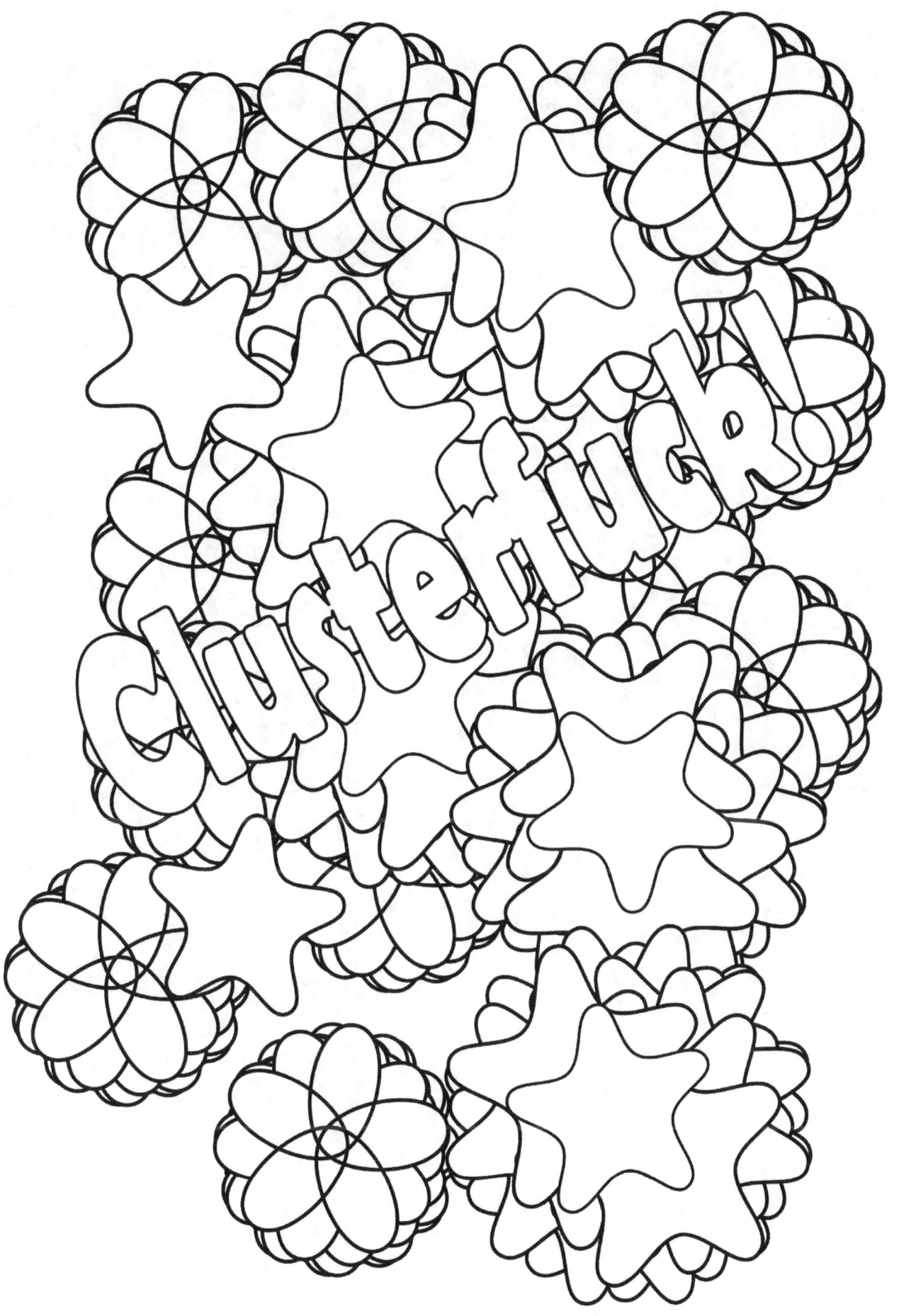

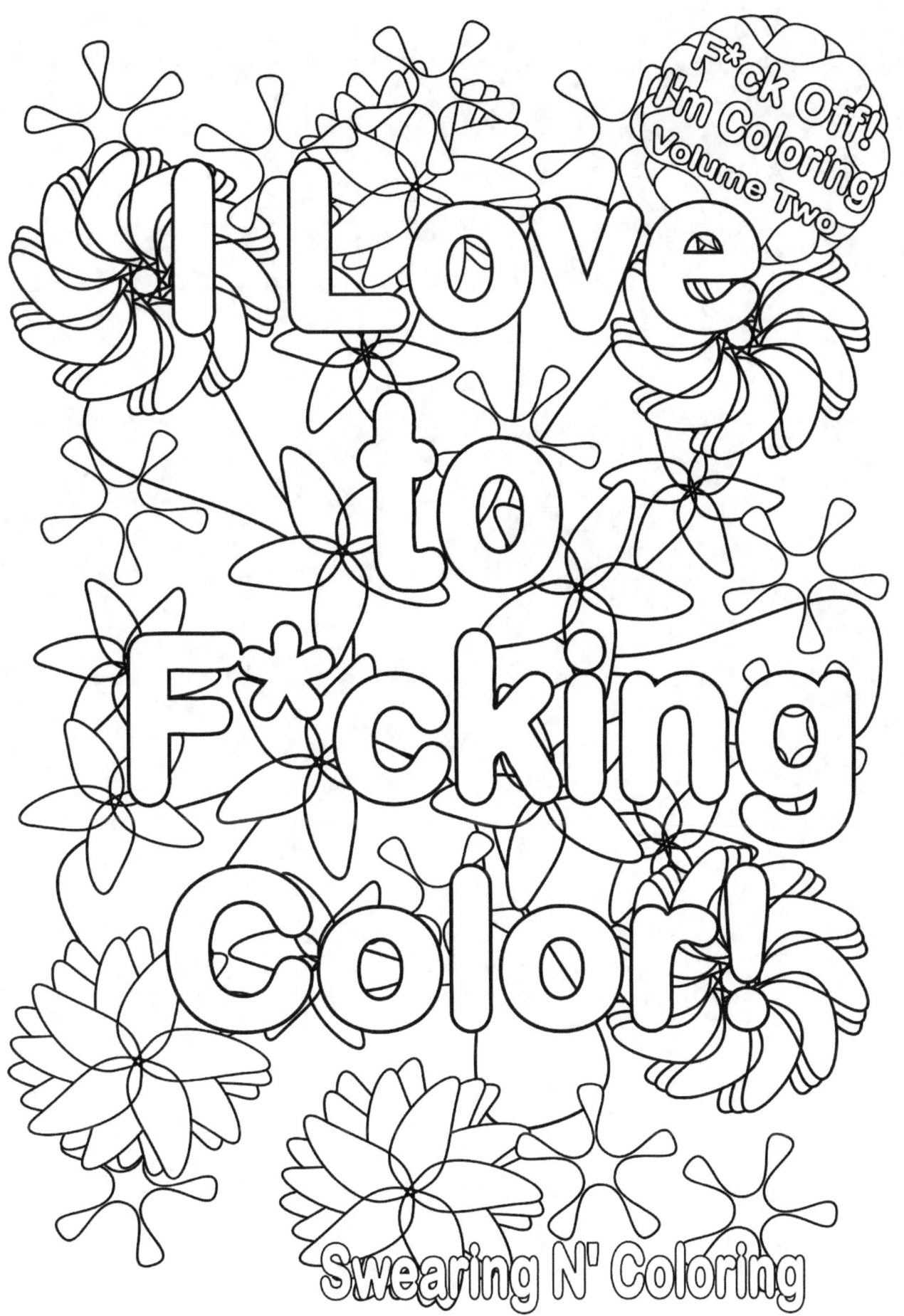

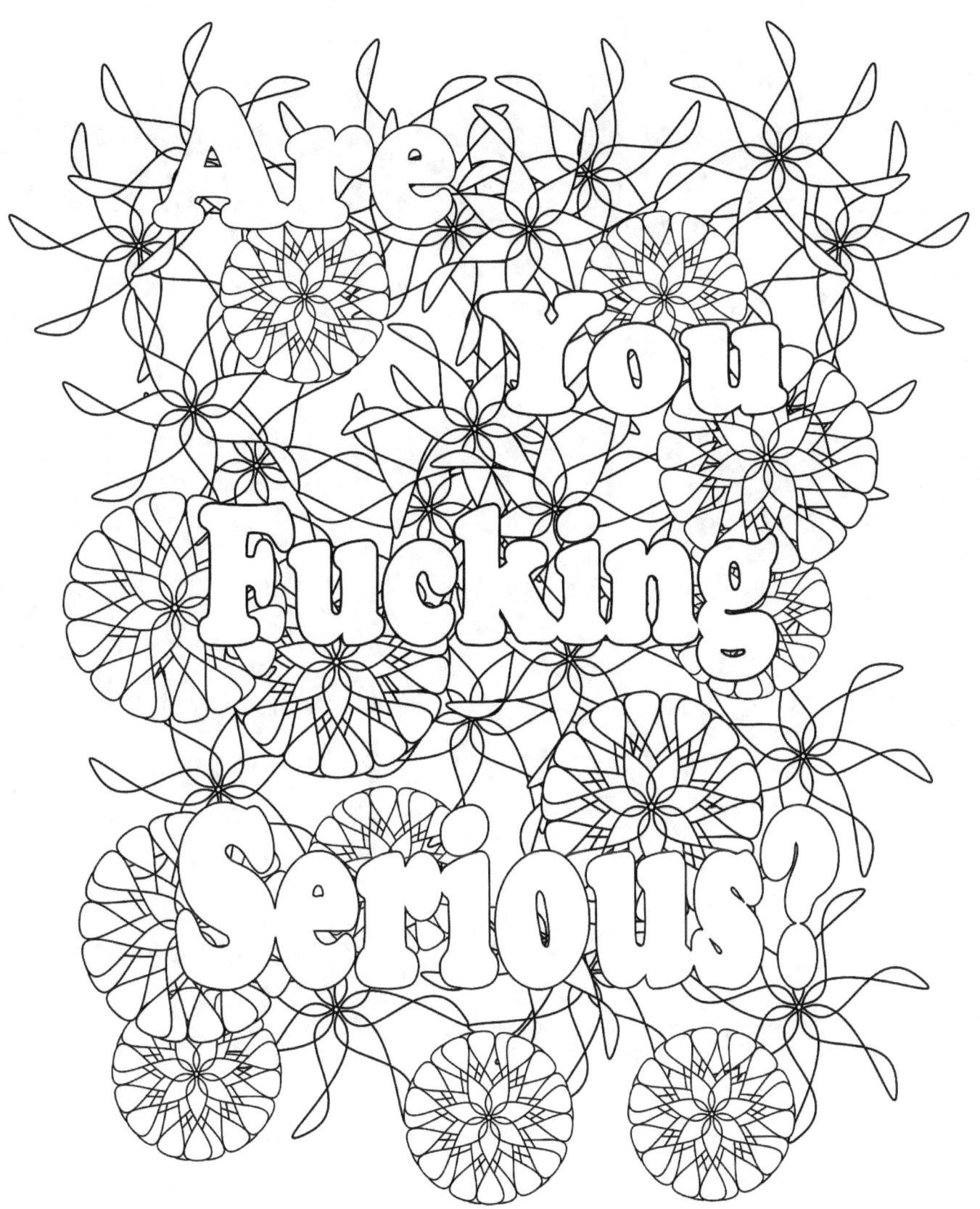

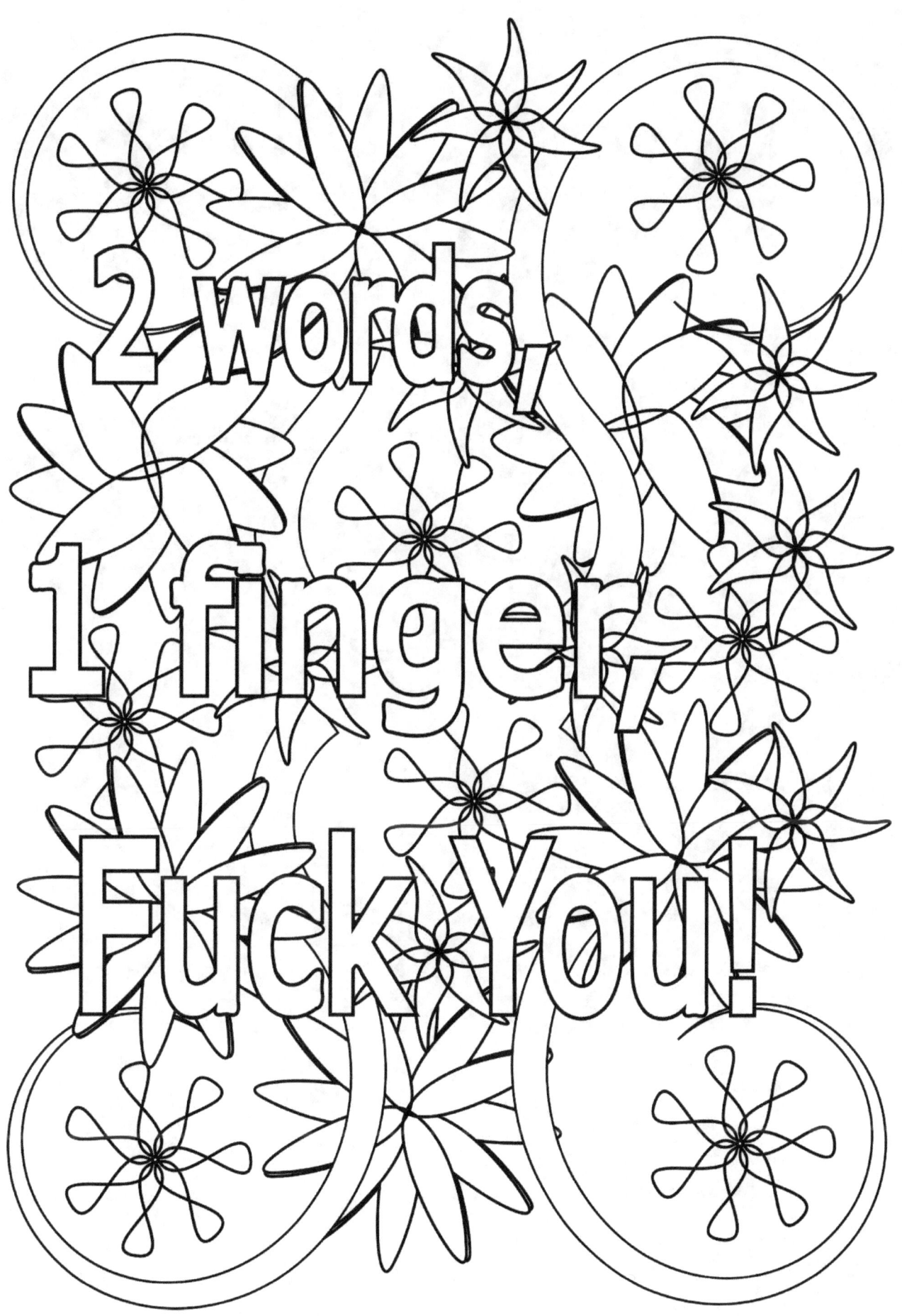

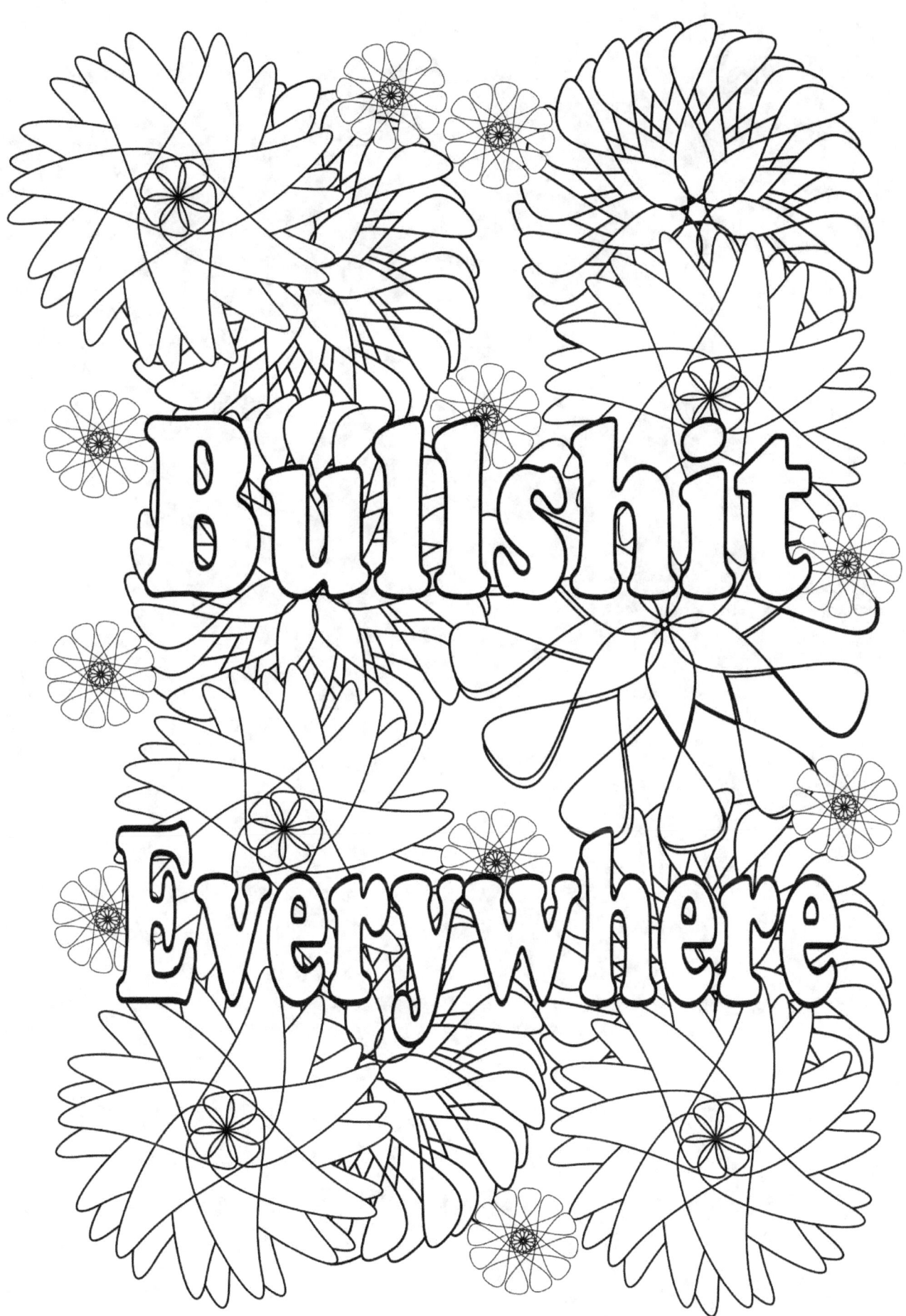

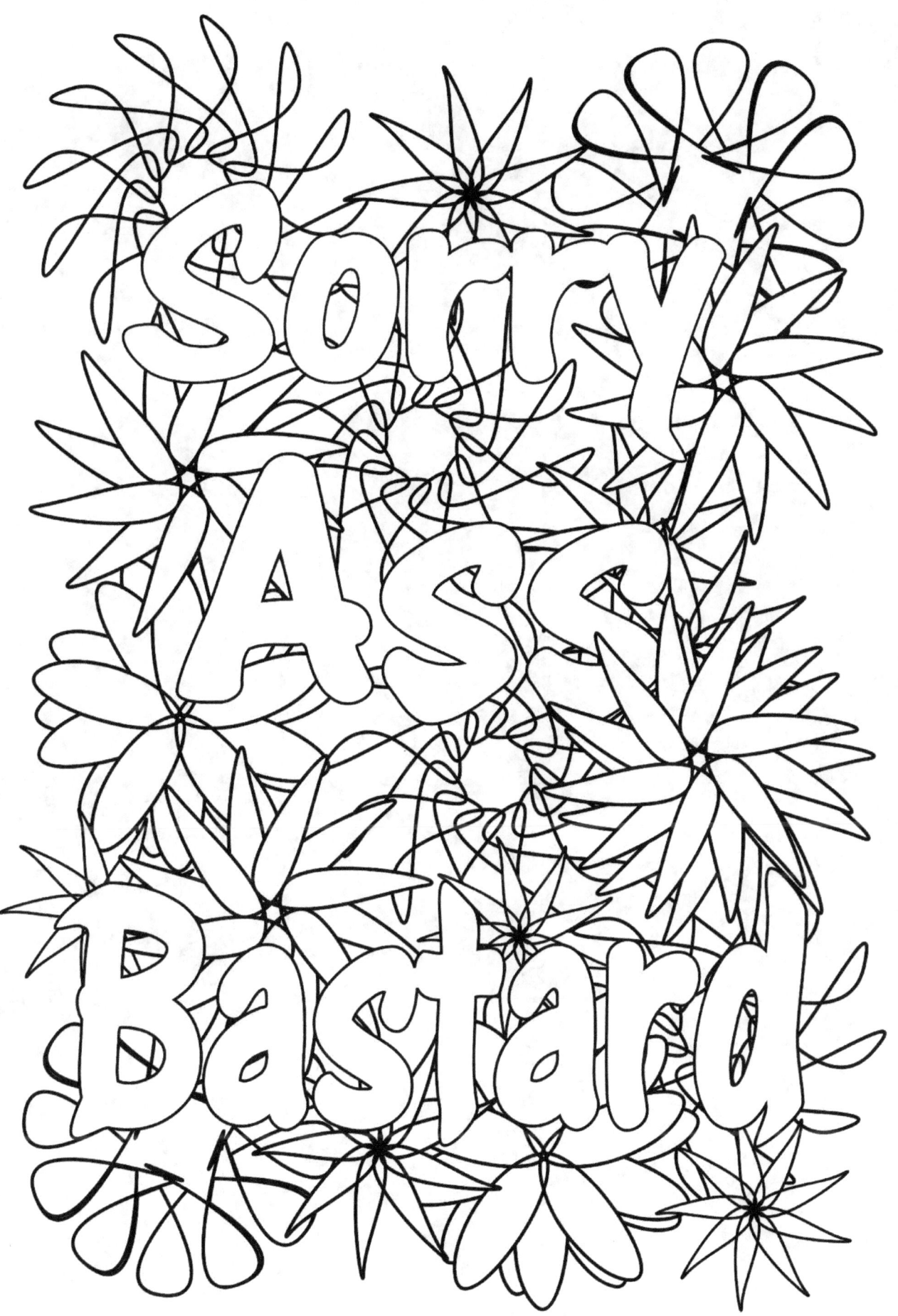

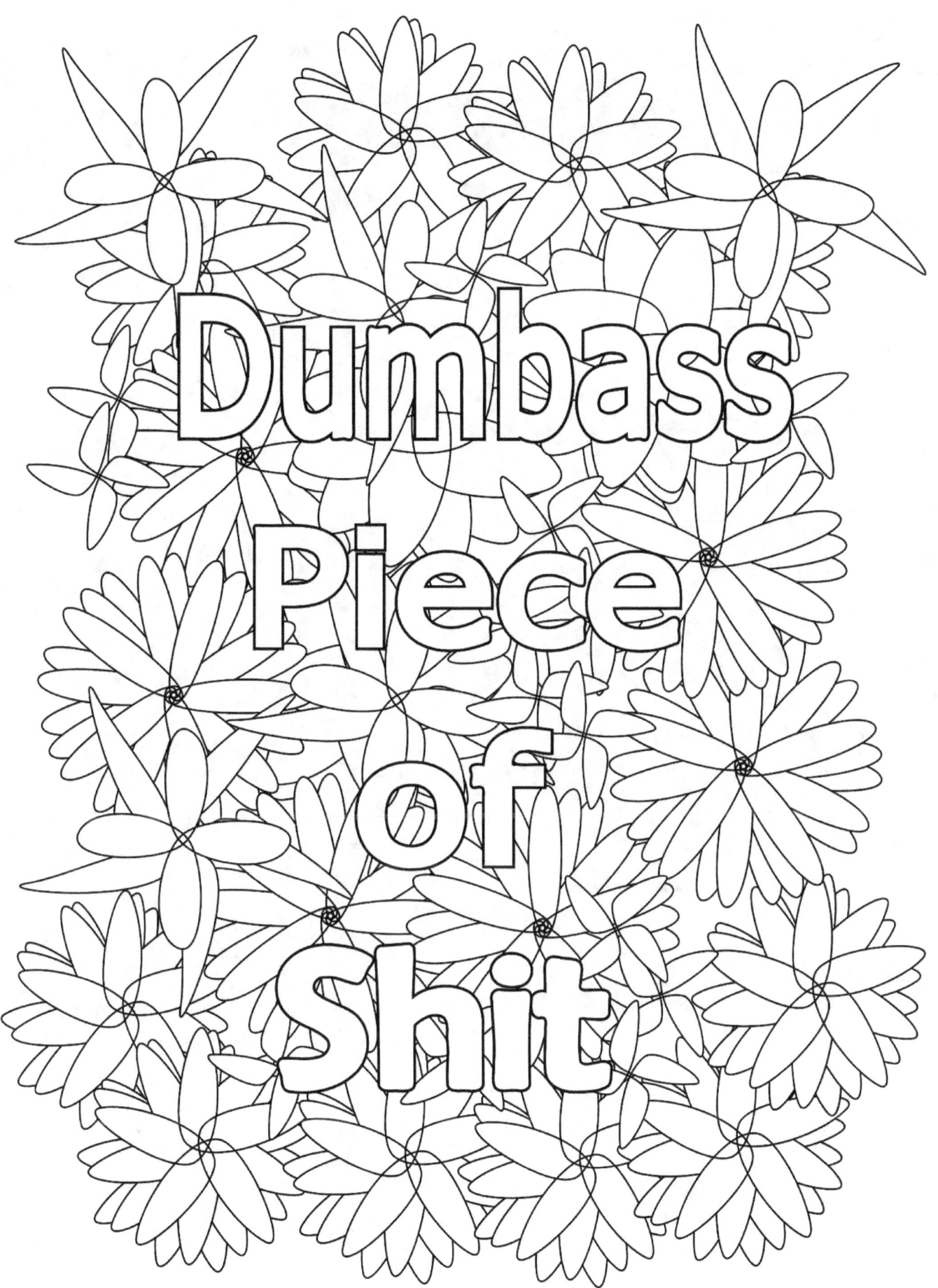

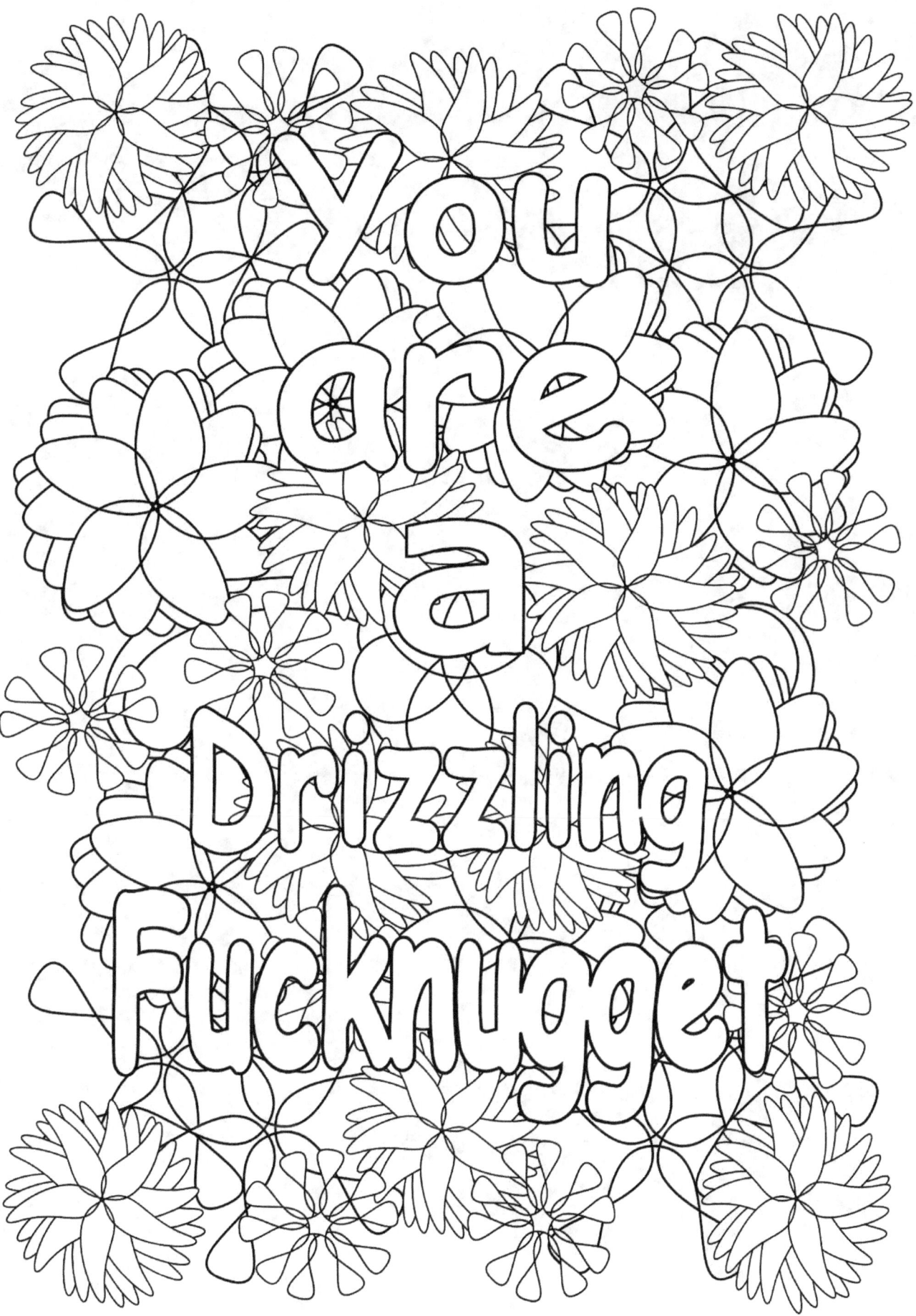

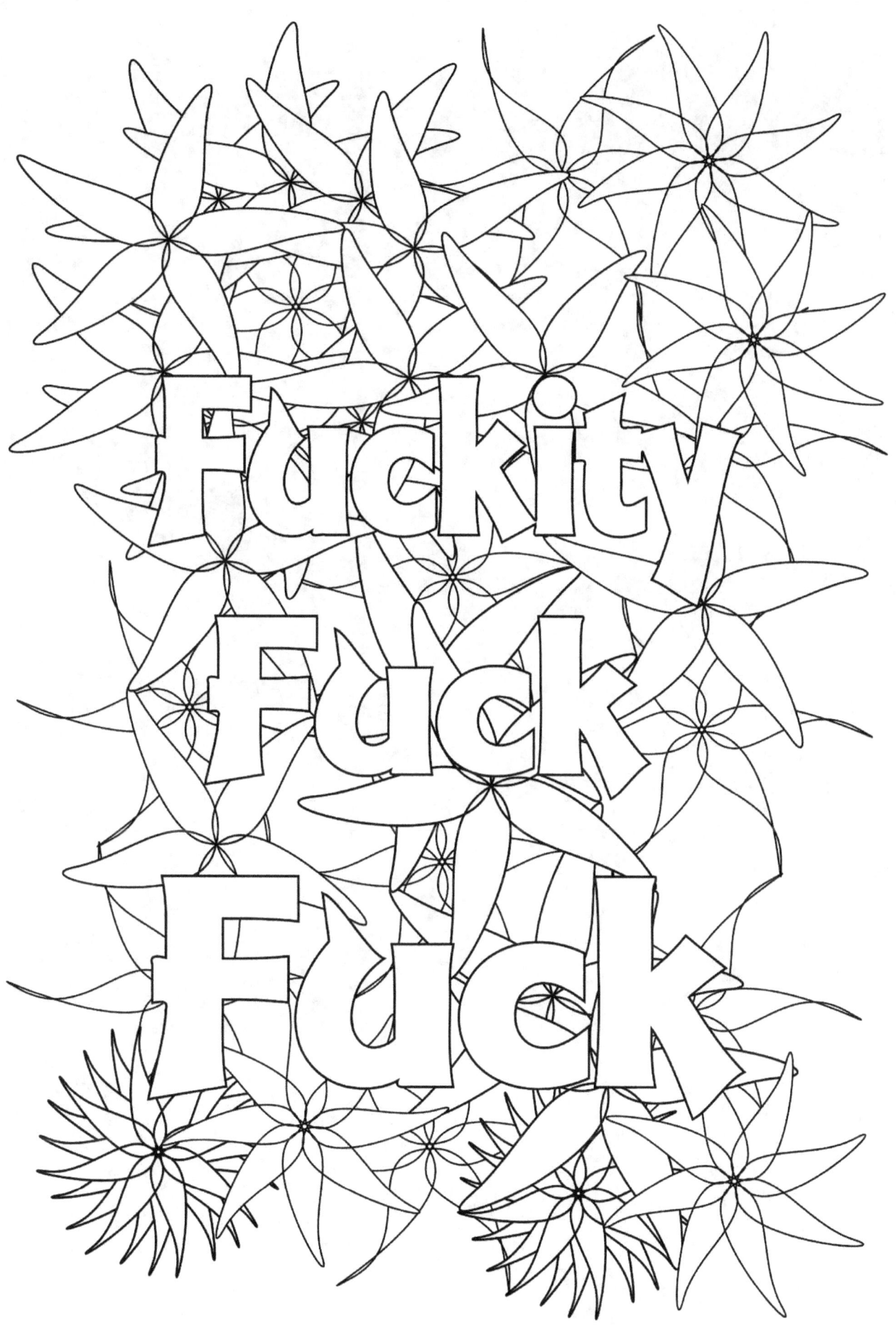

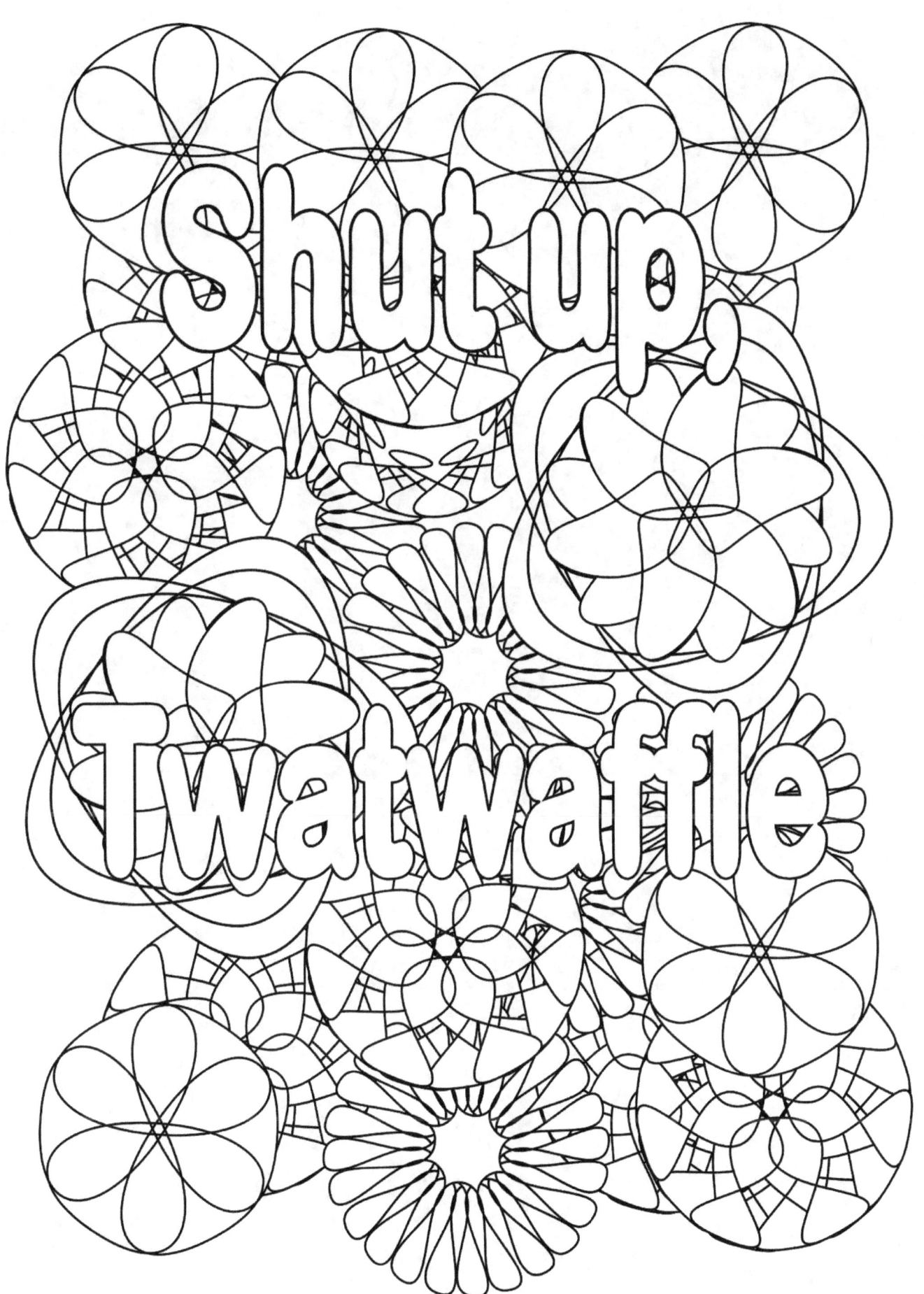

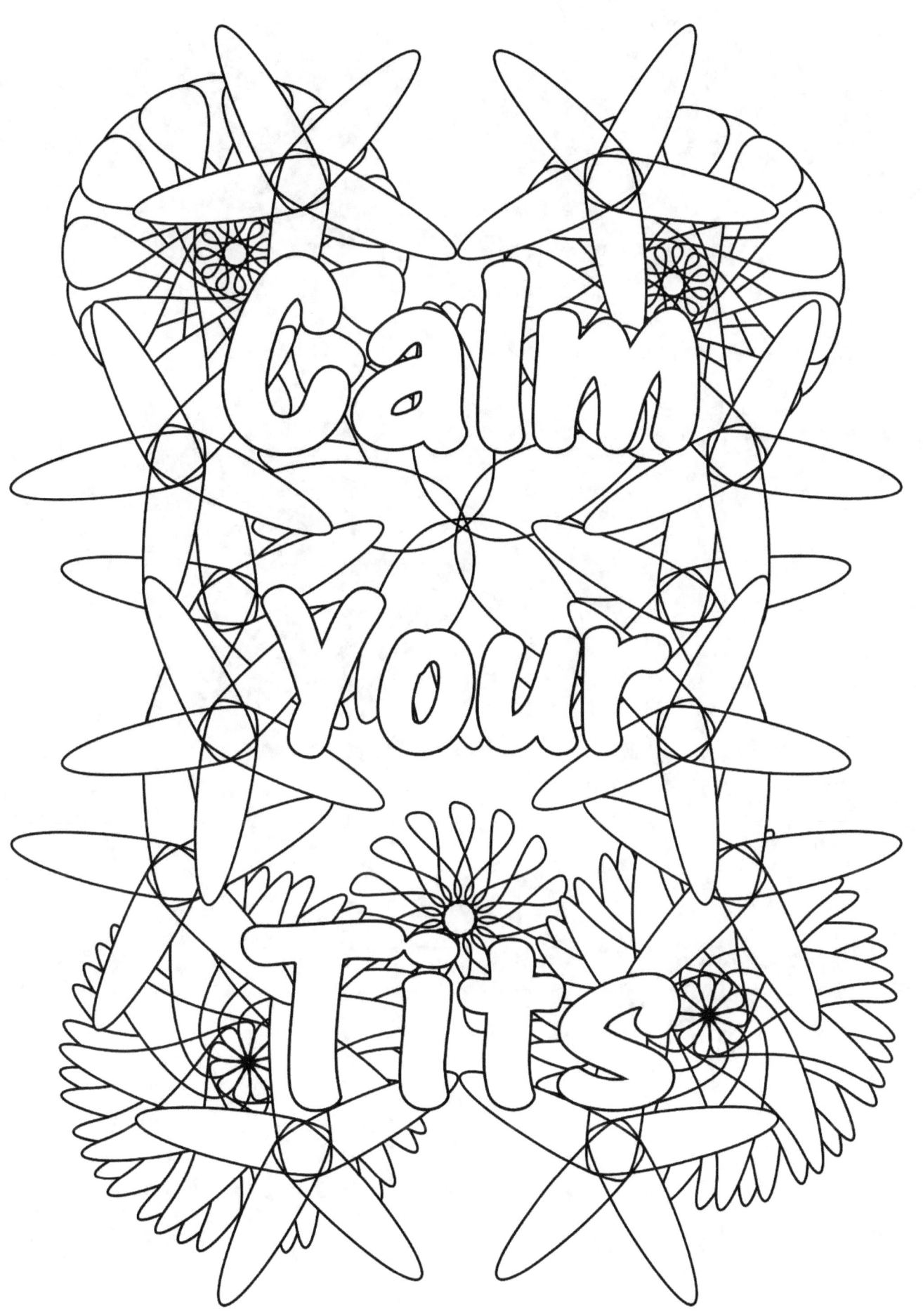

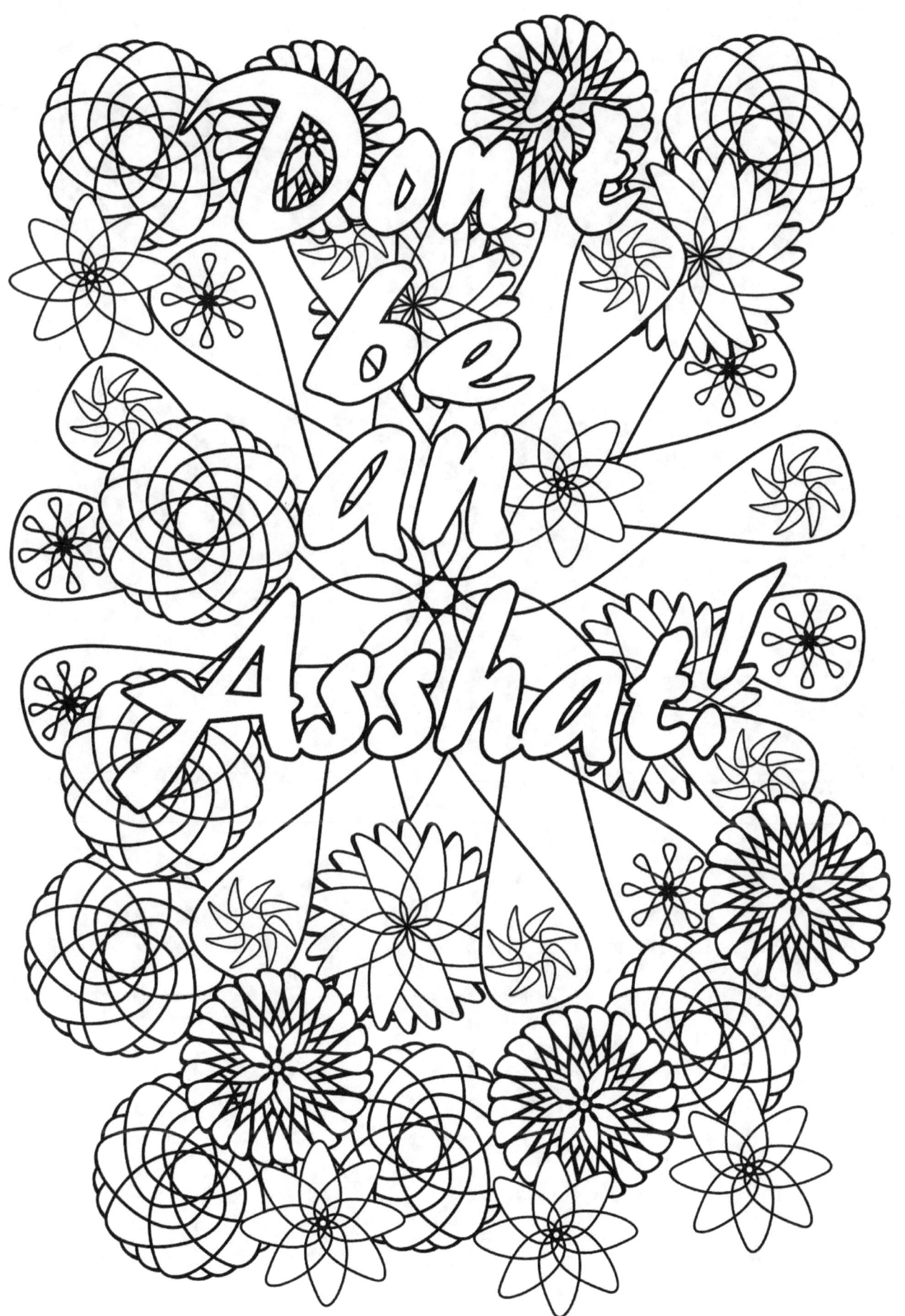

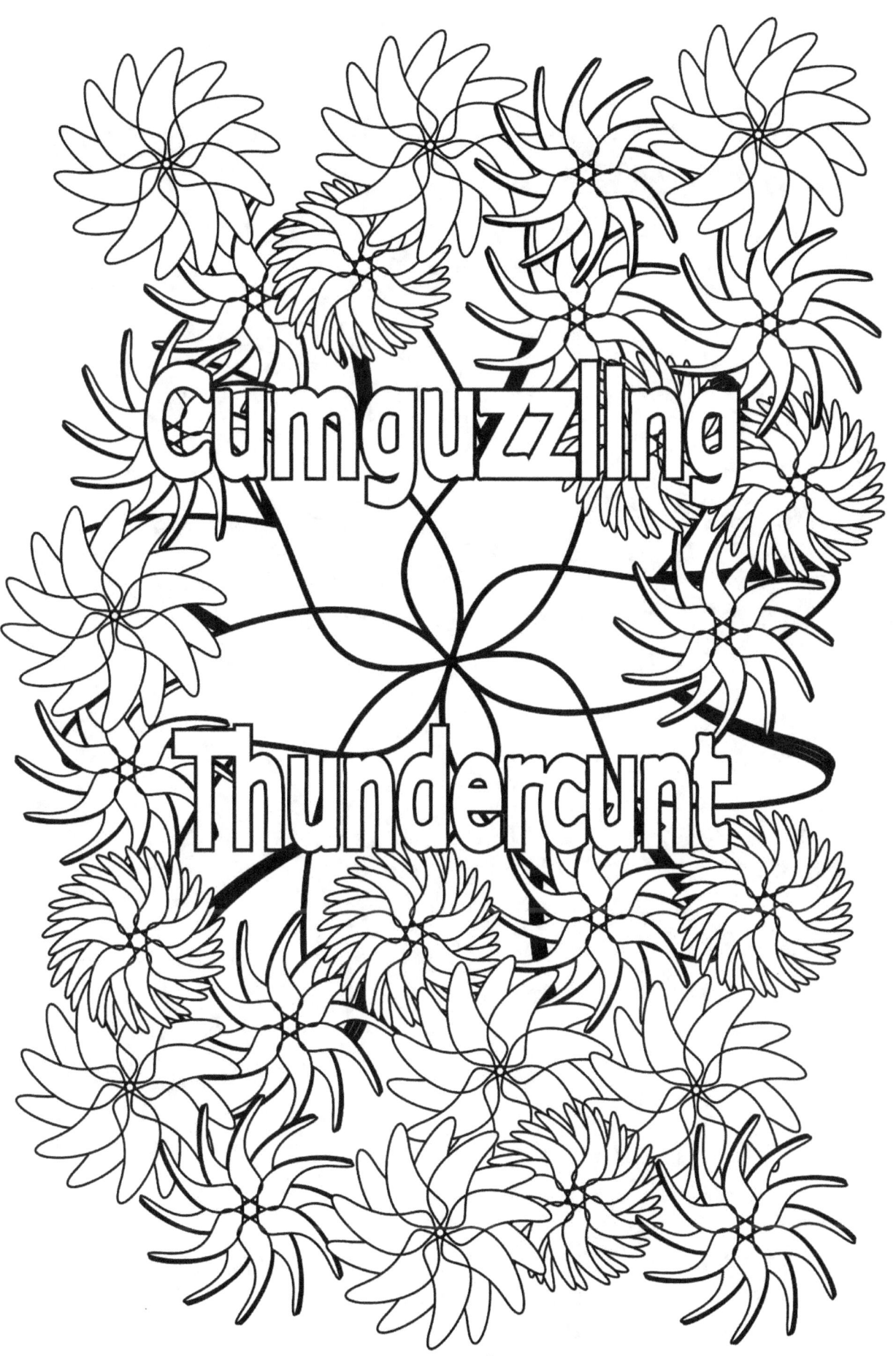

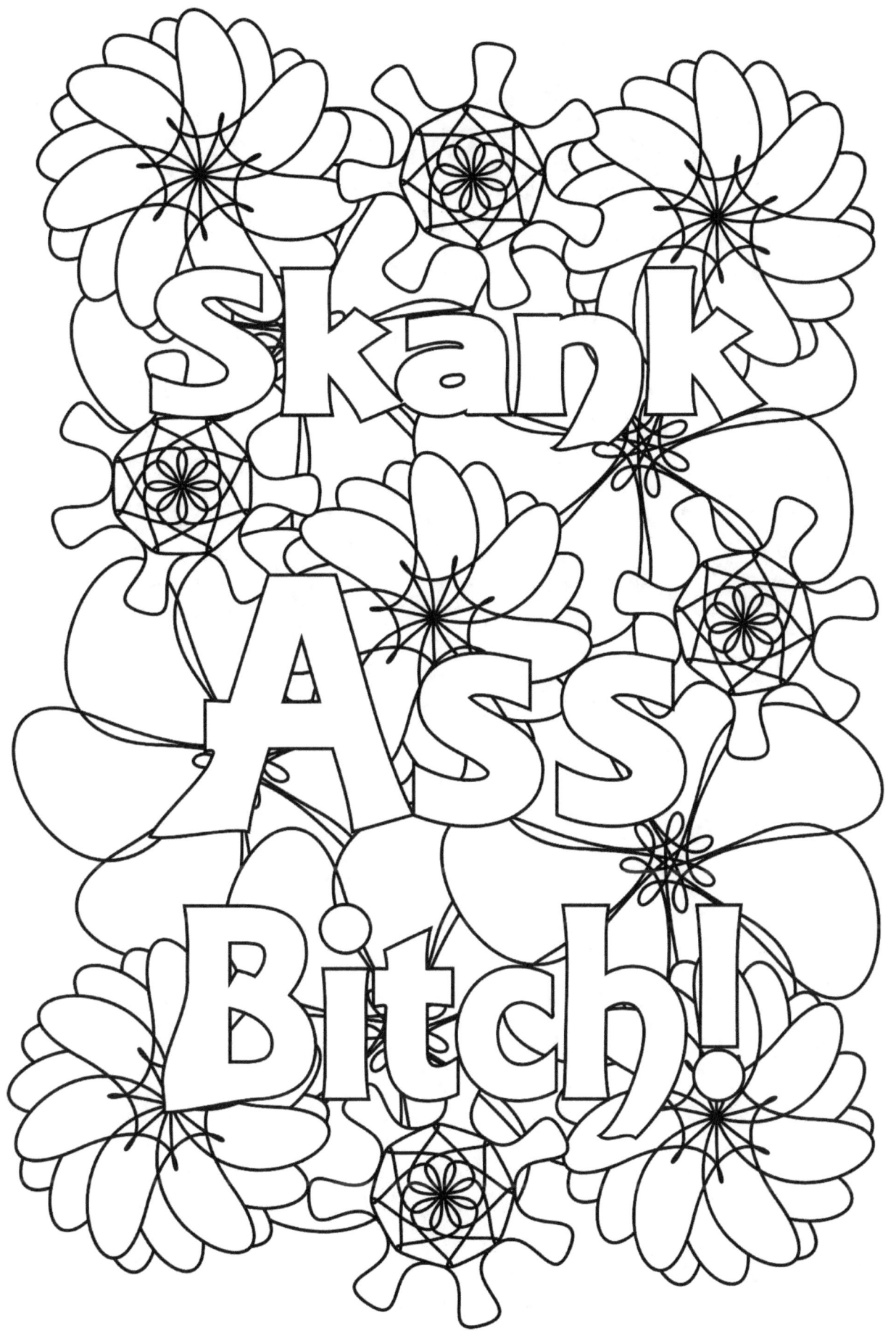

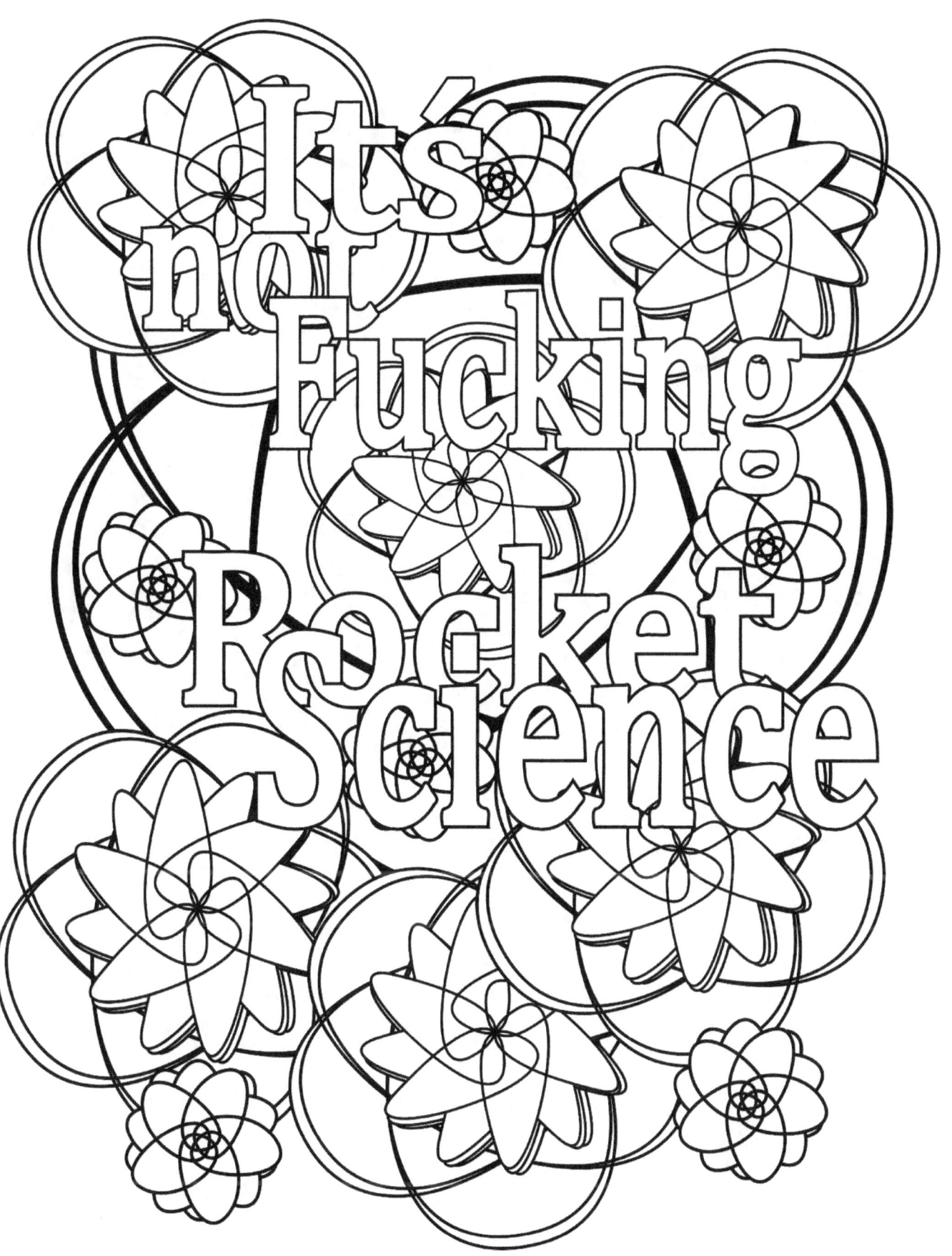

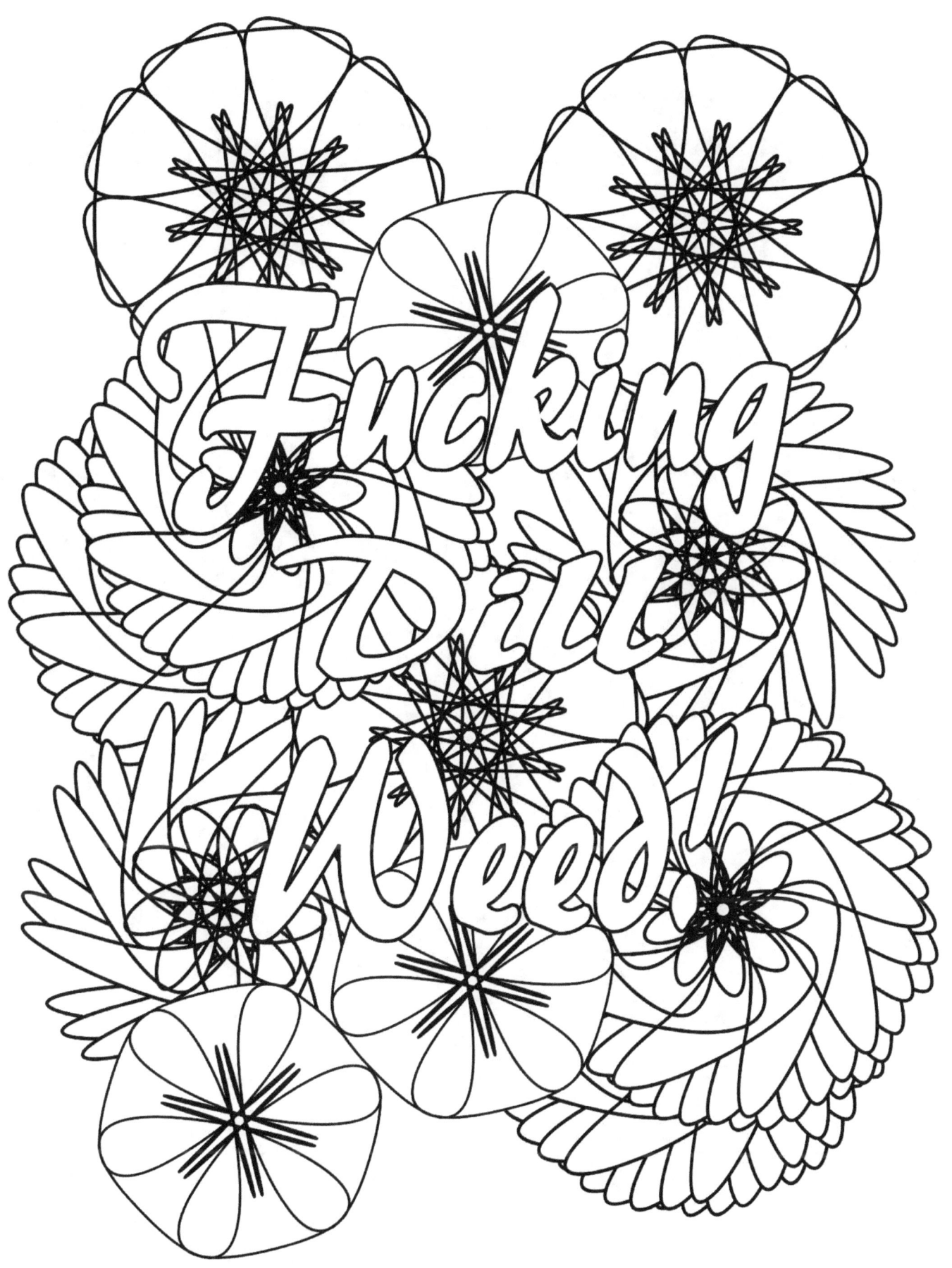

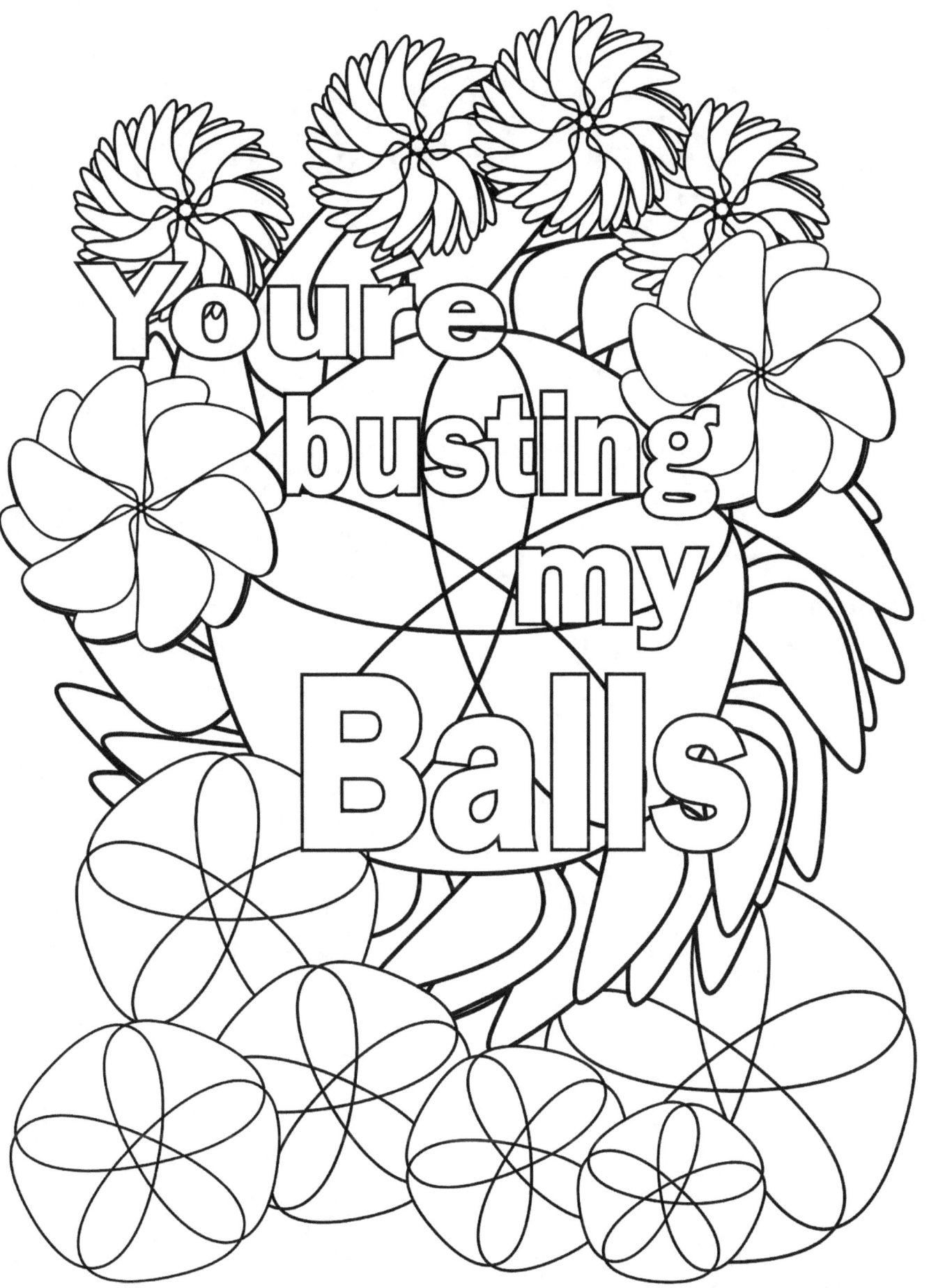

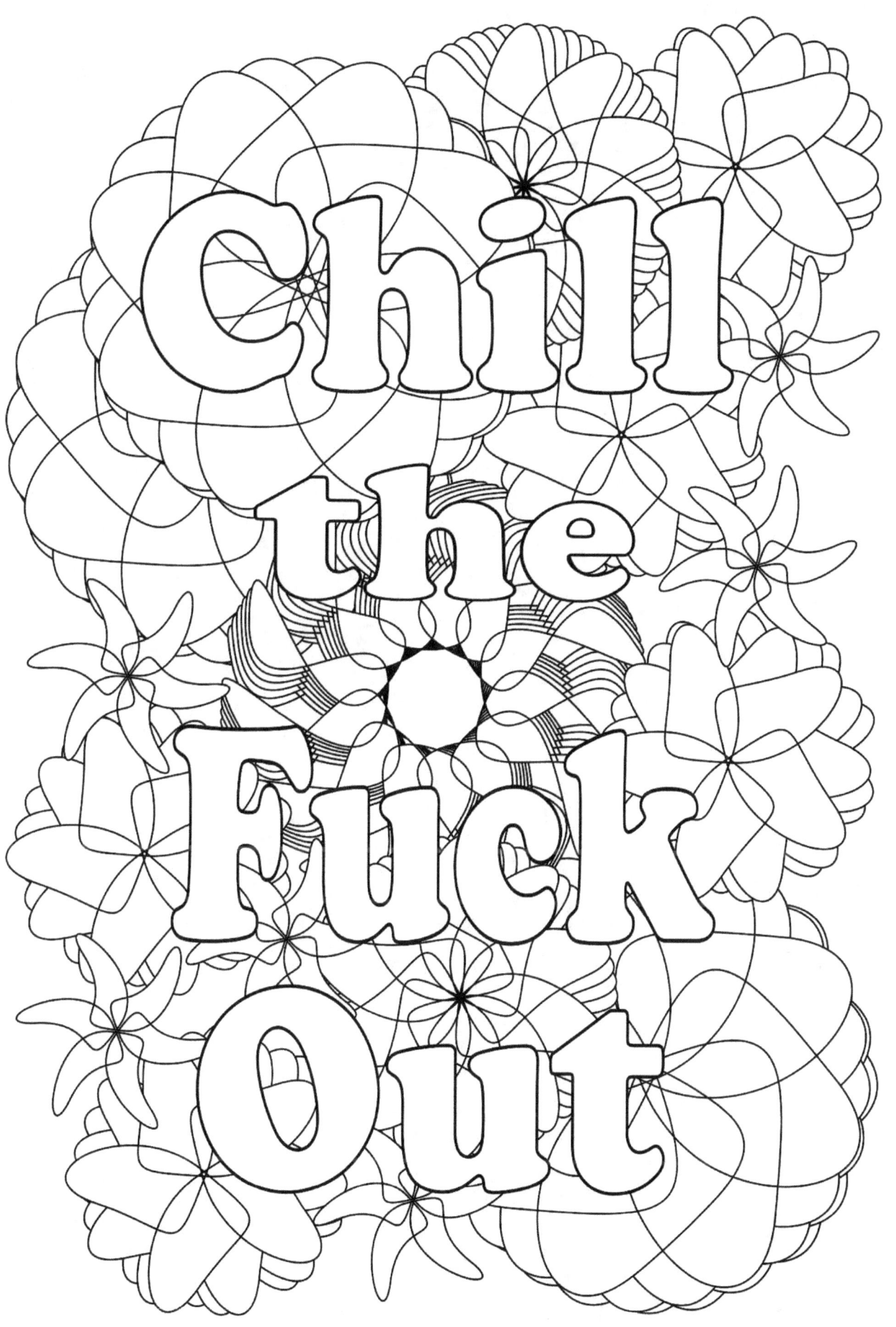

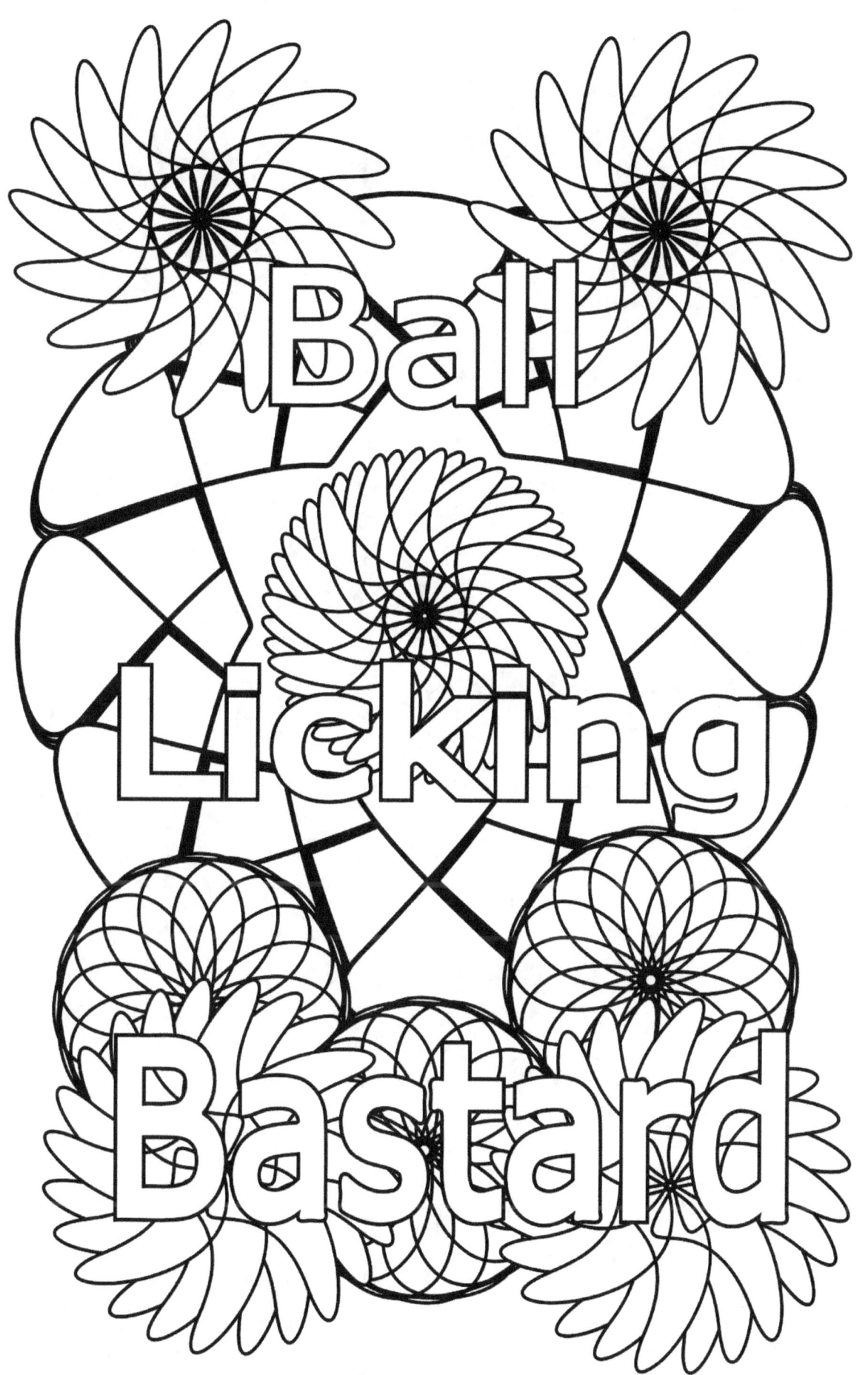

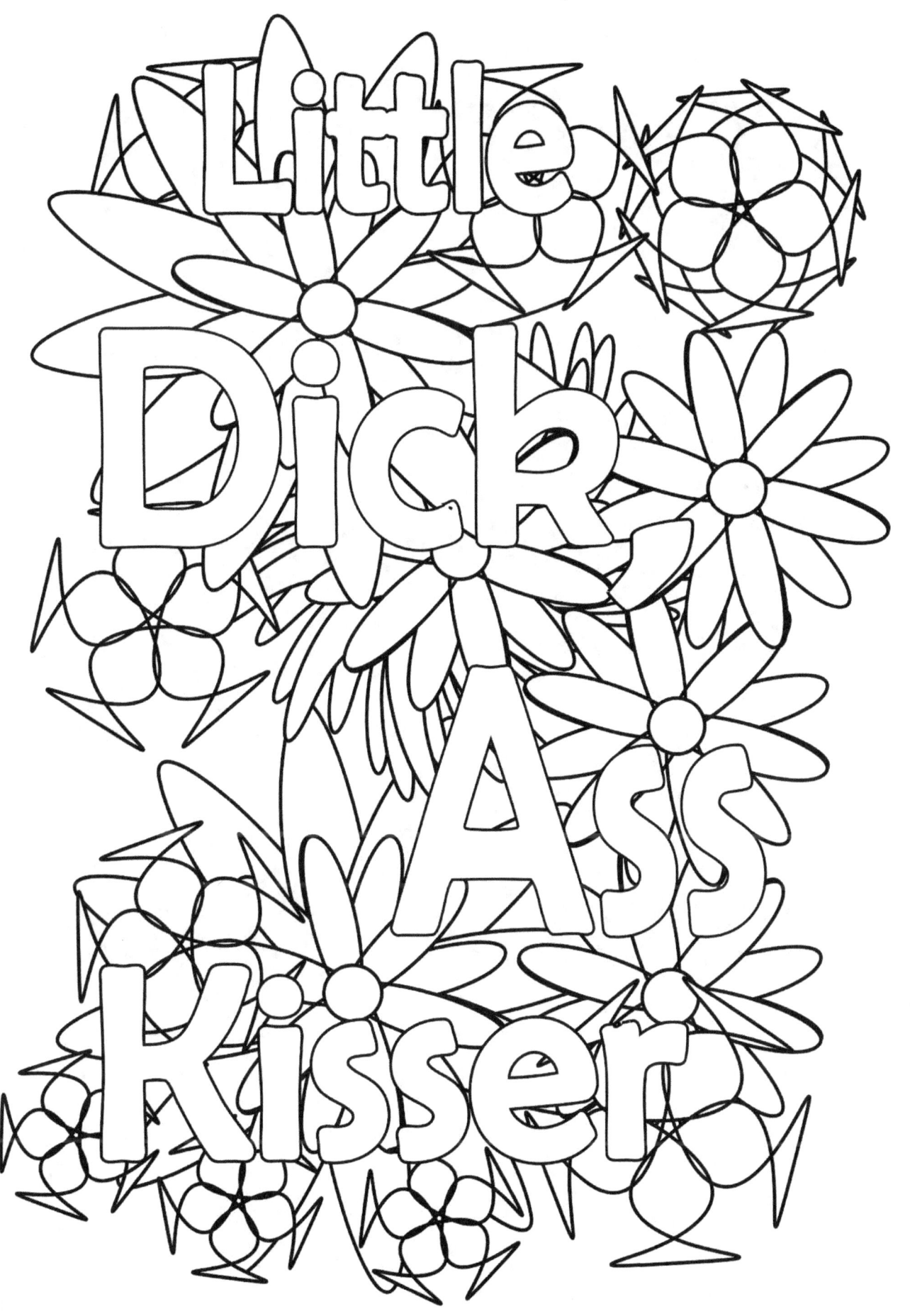

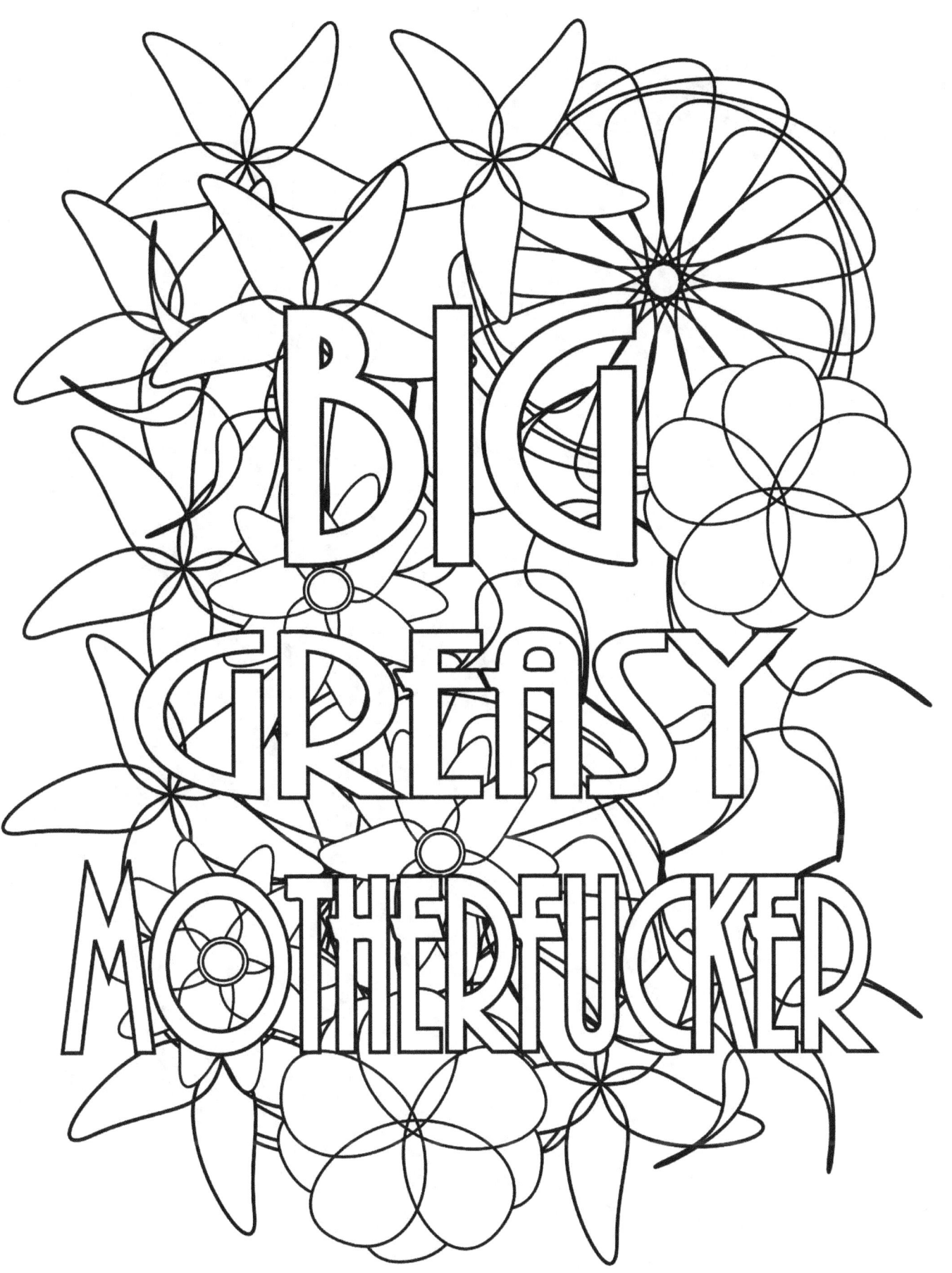

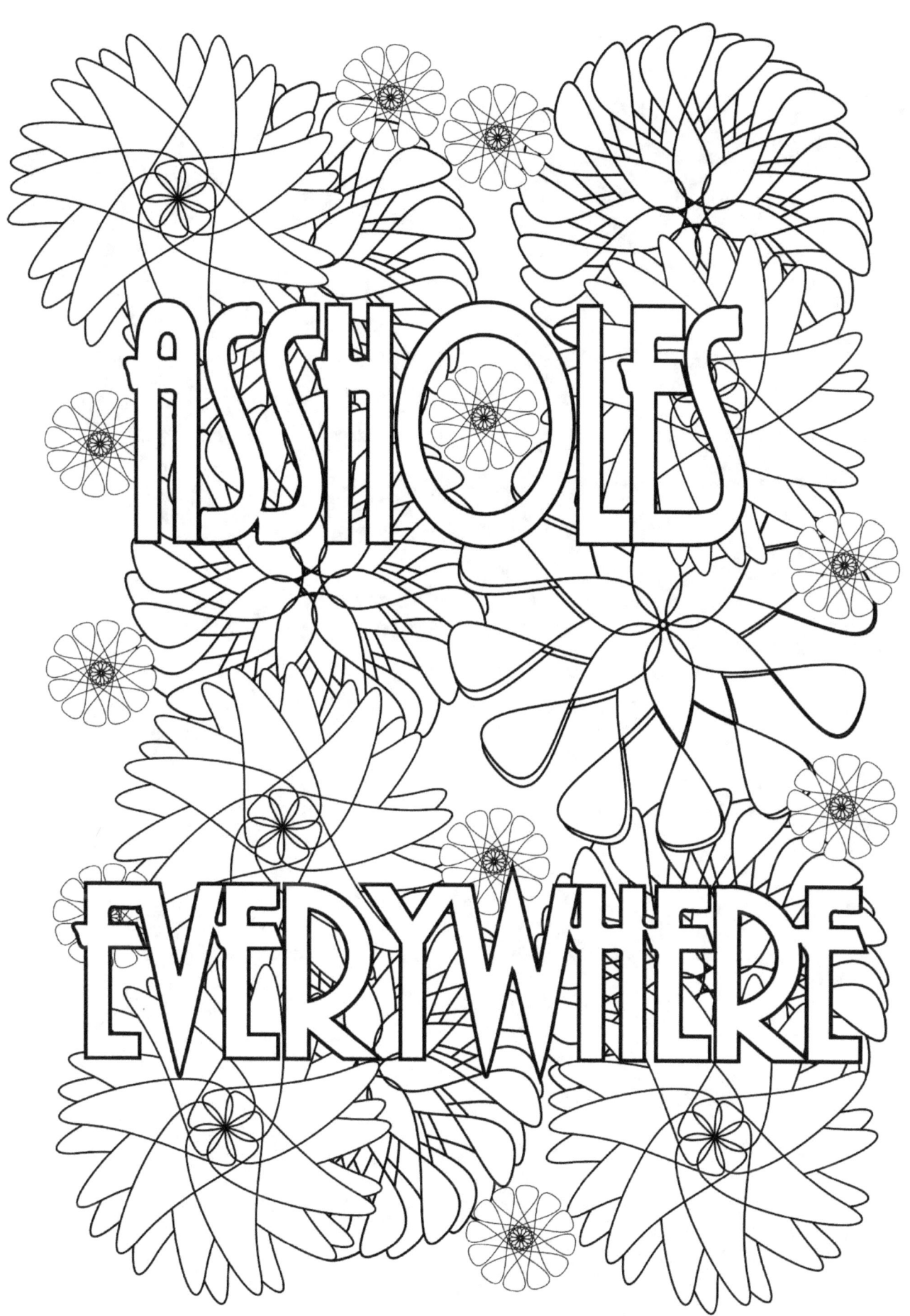

I May Go to Hell, But I'll be Coloring on the Way Down!

A Swear Word Adult Coloring Book
By Swearing N' Coloring

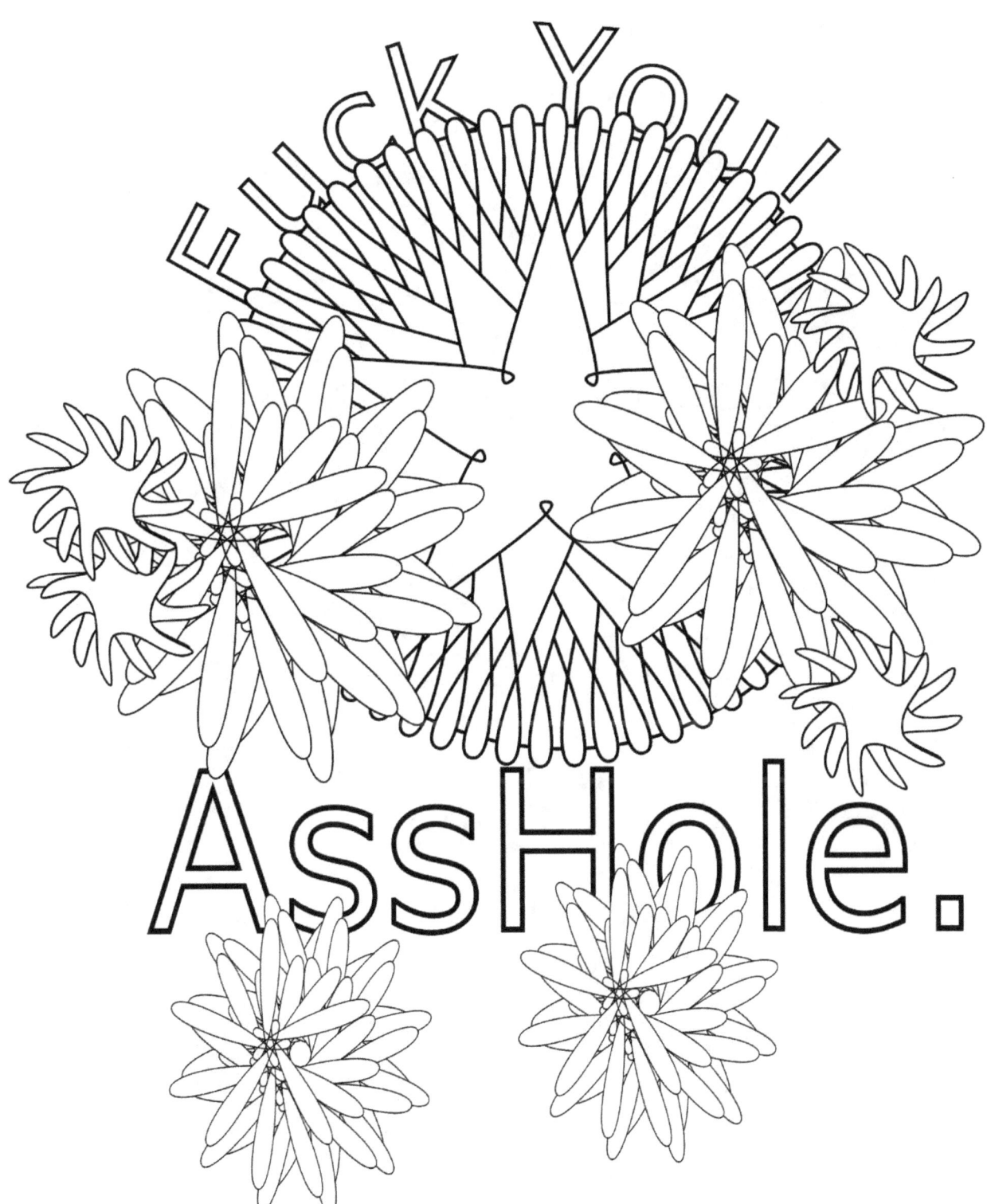

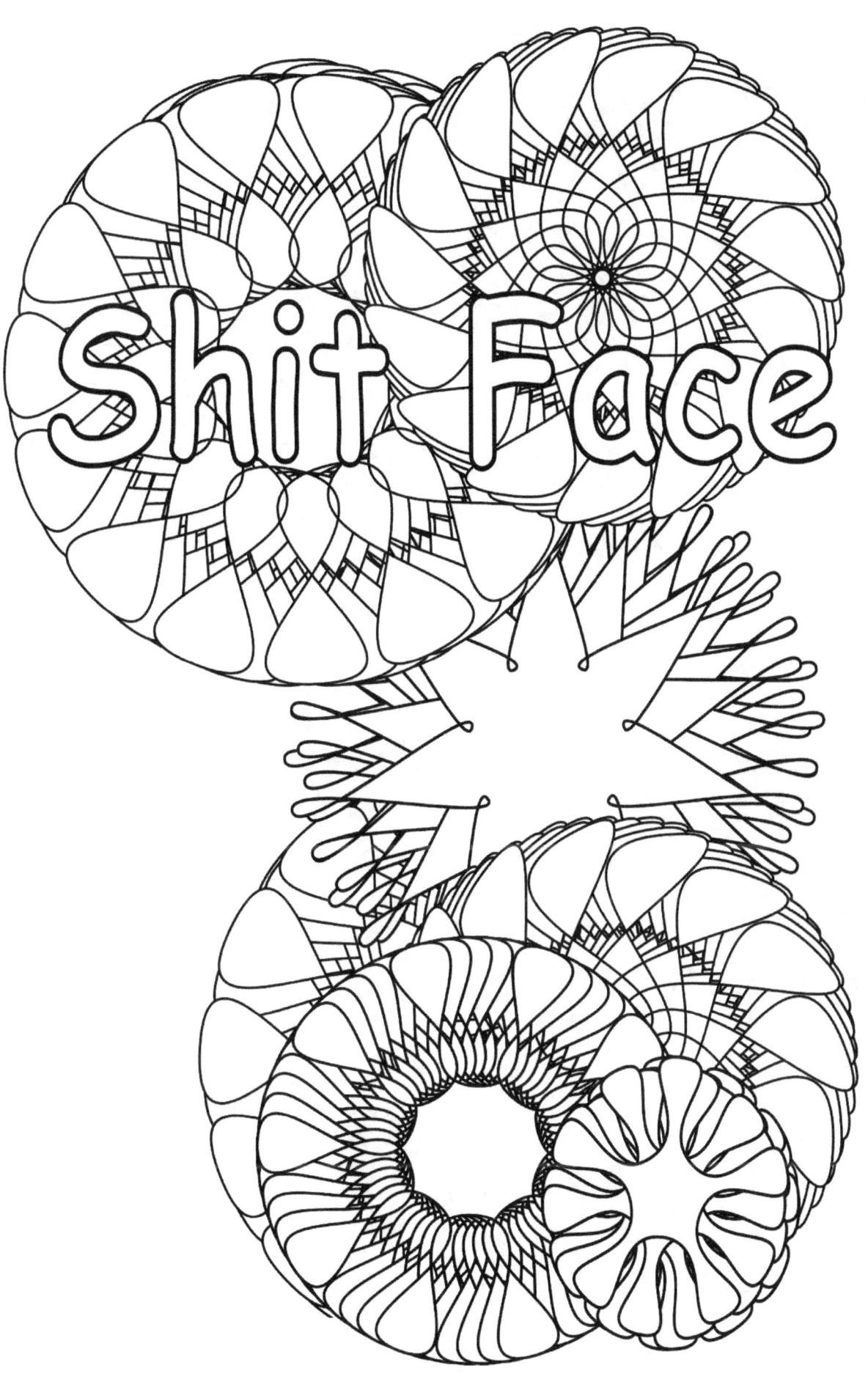

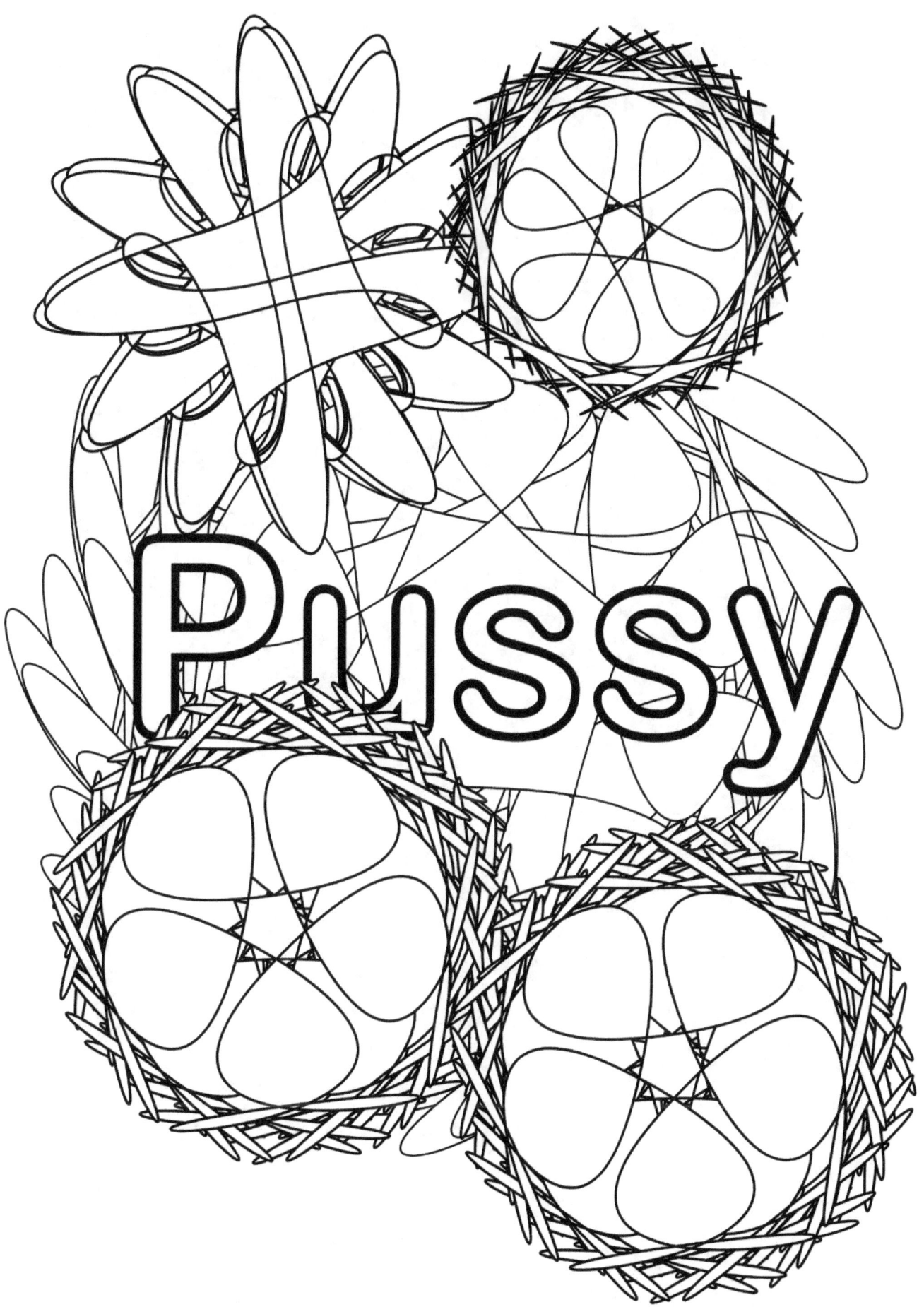

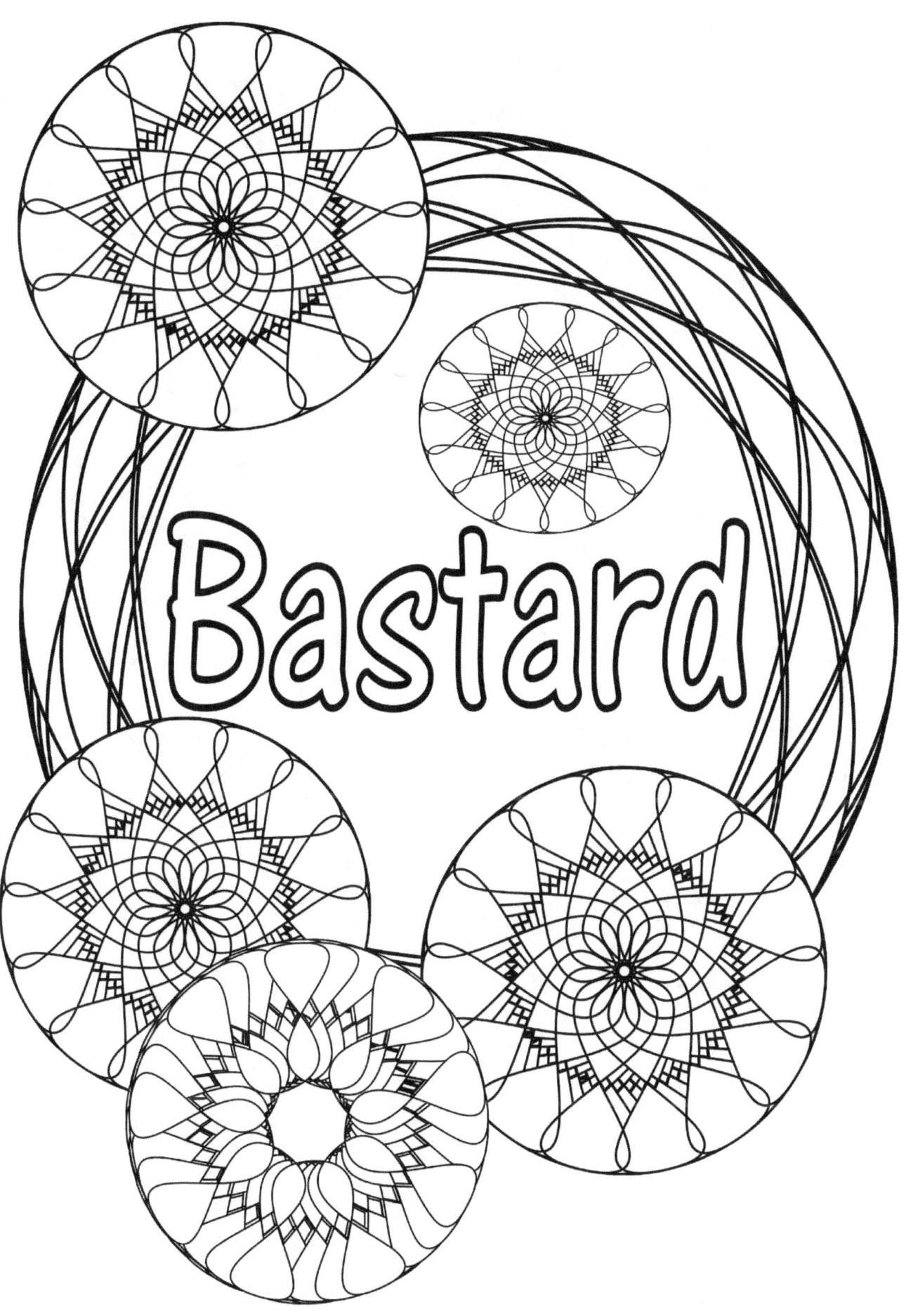

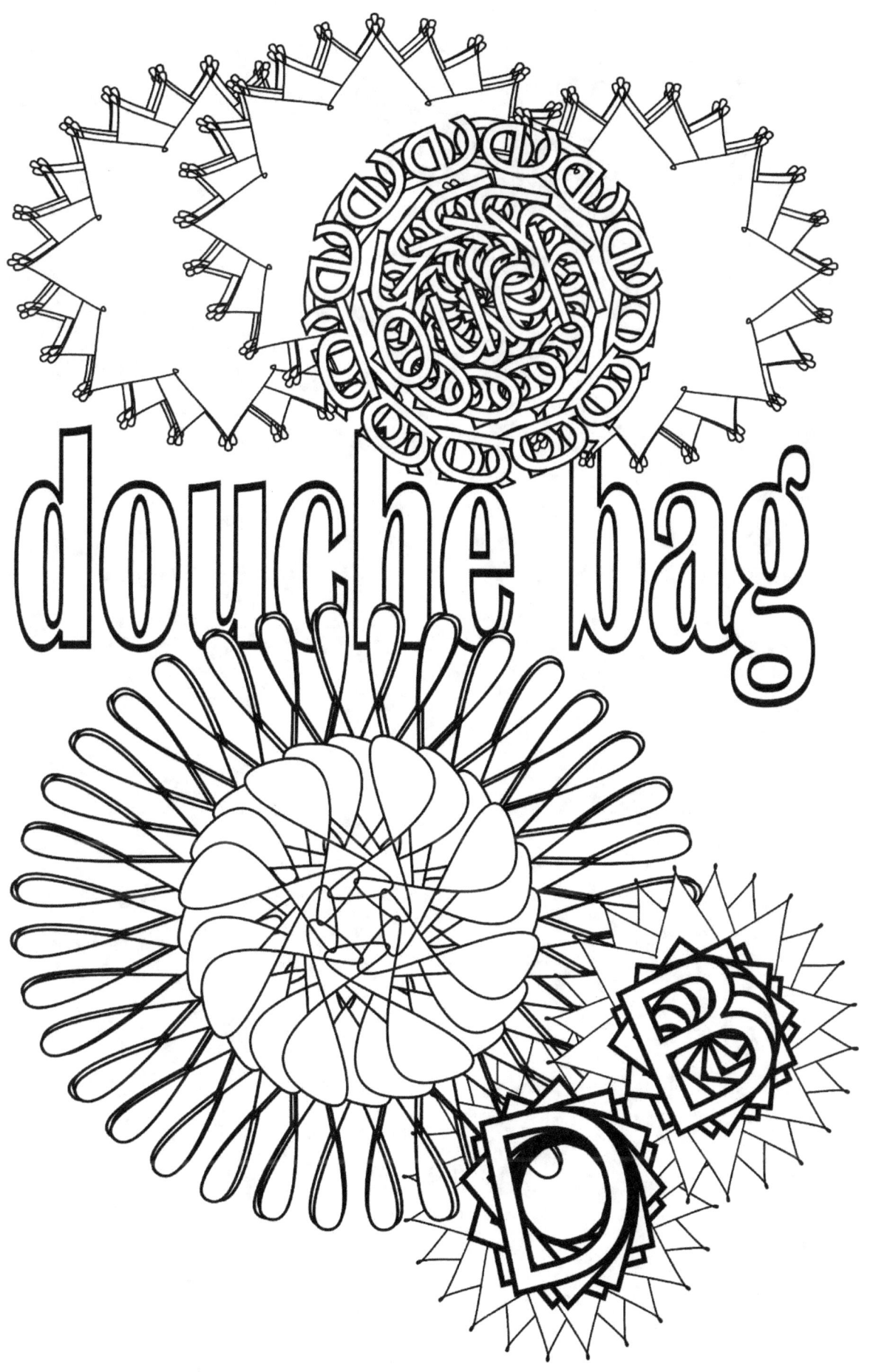

douche bag

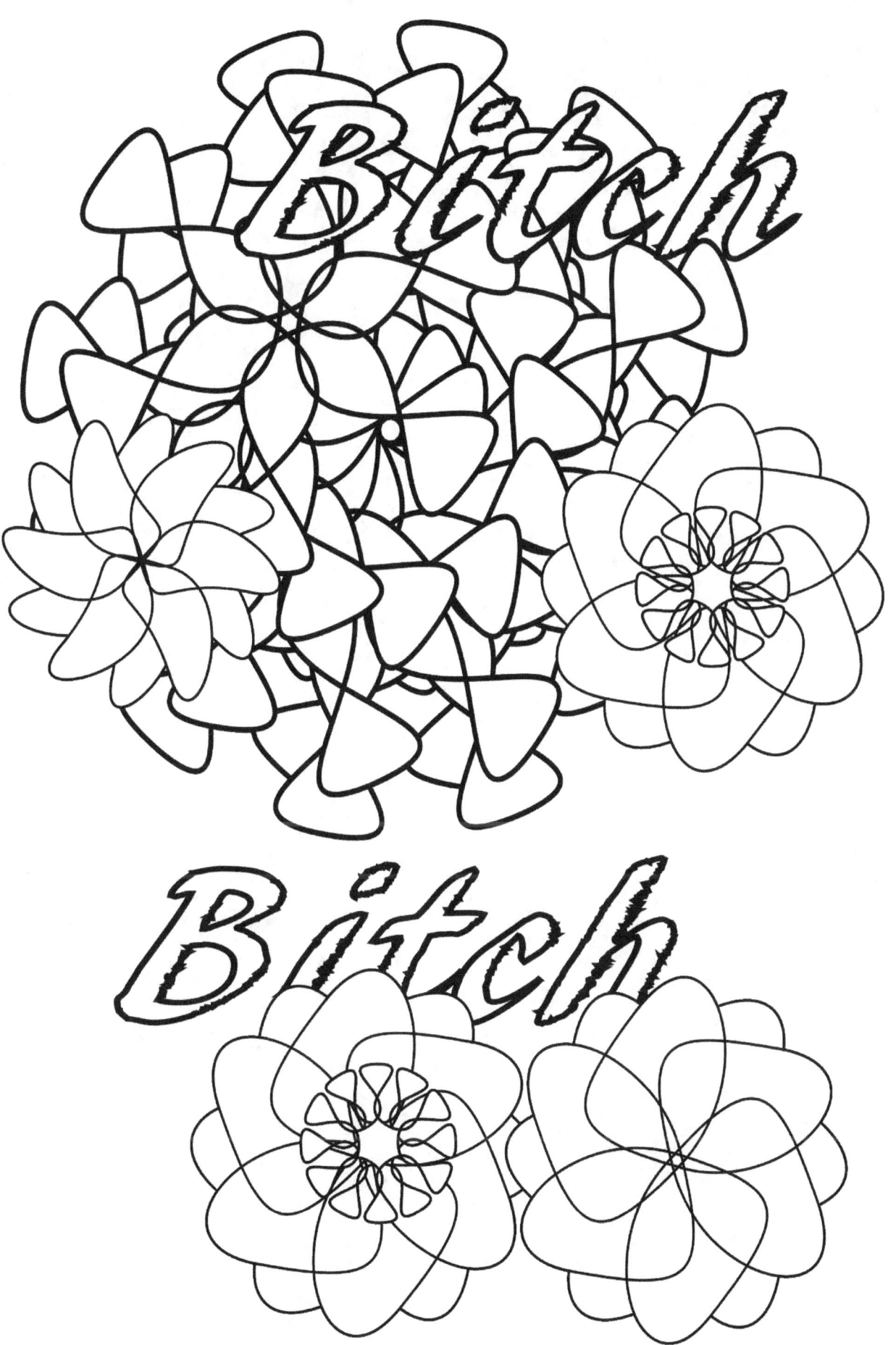

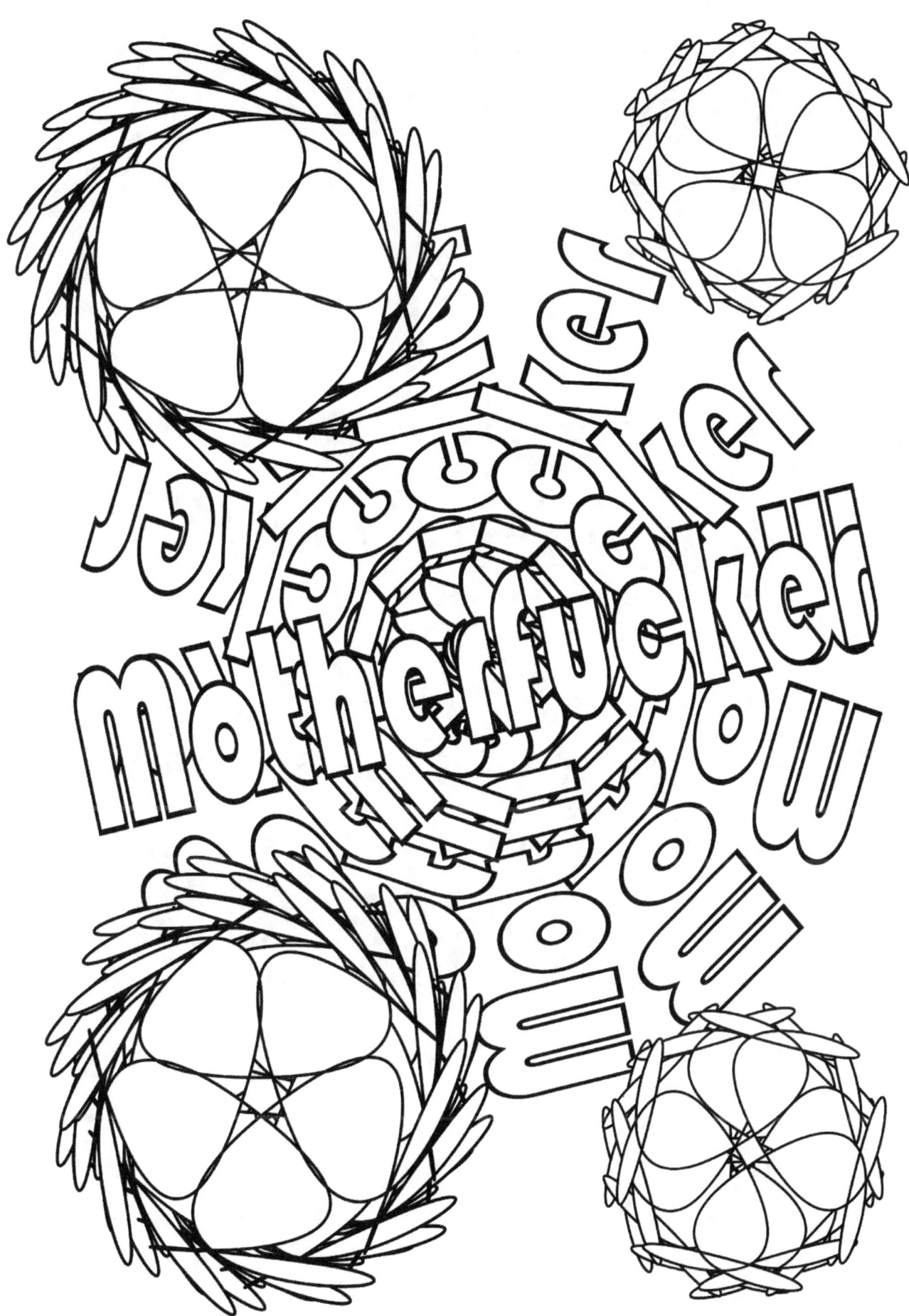

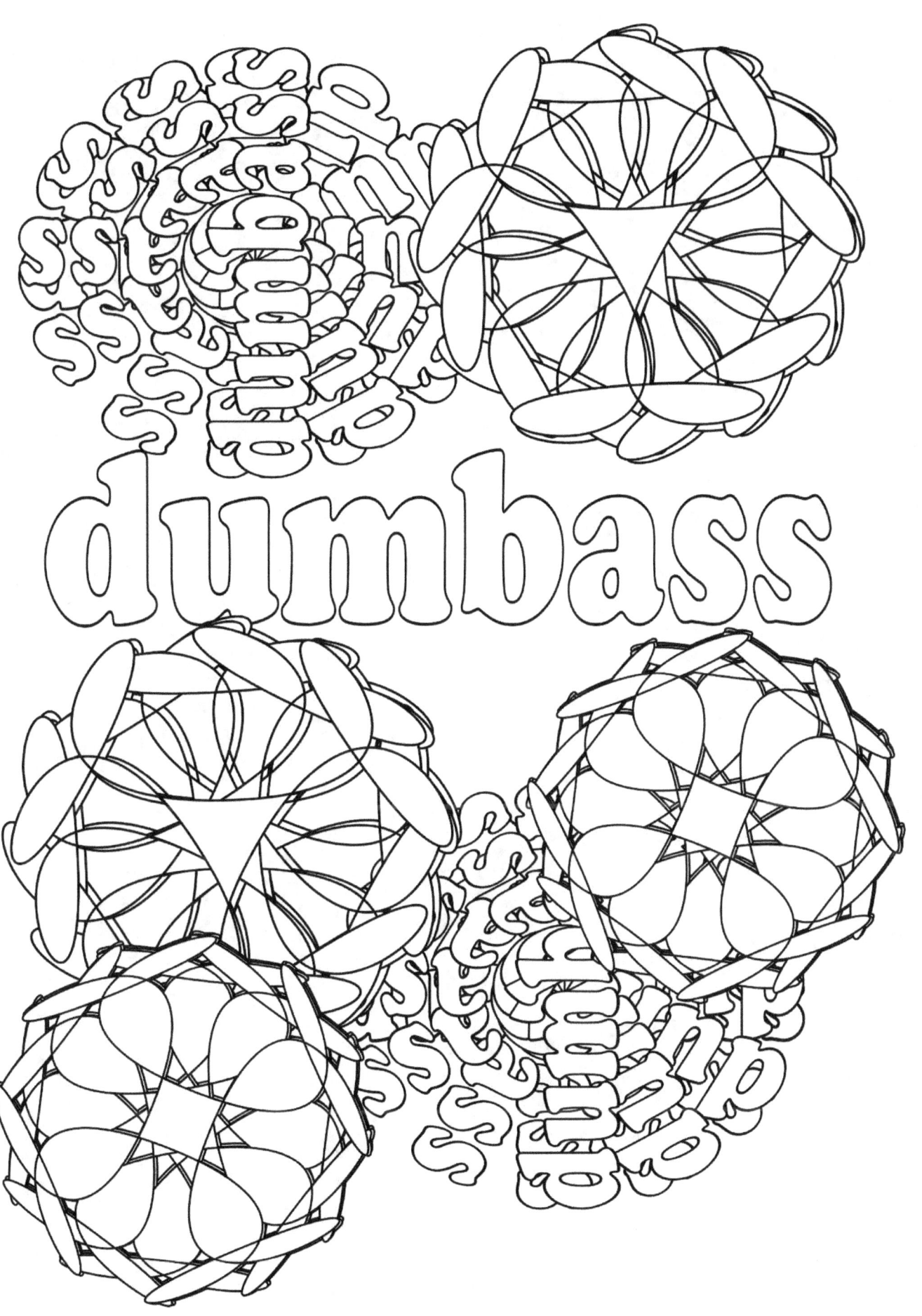

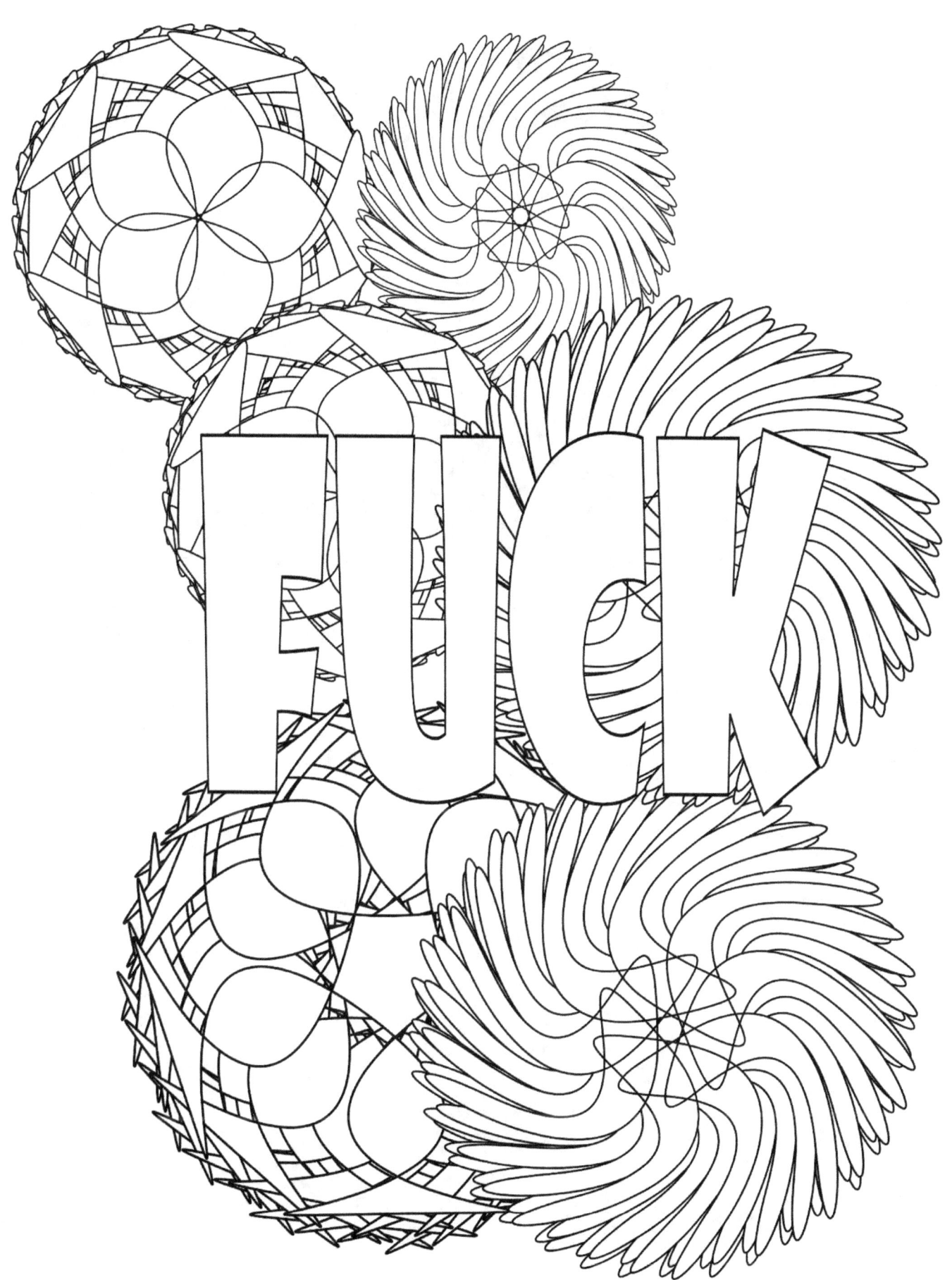

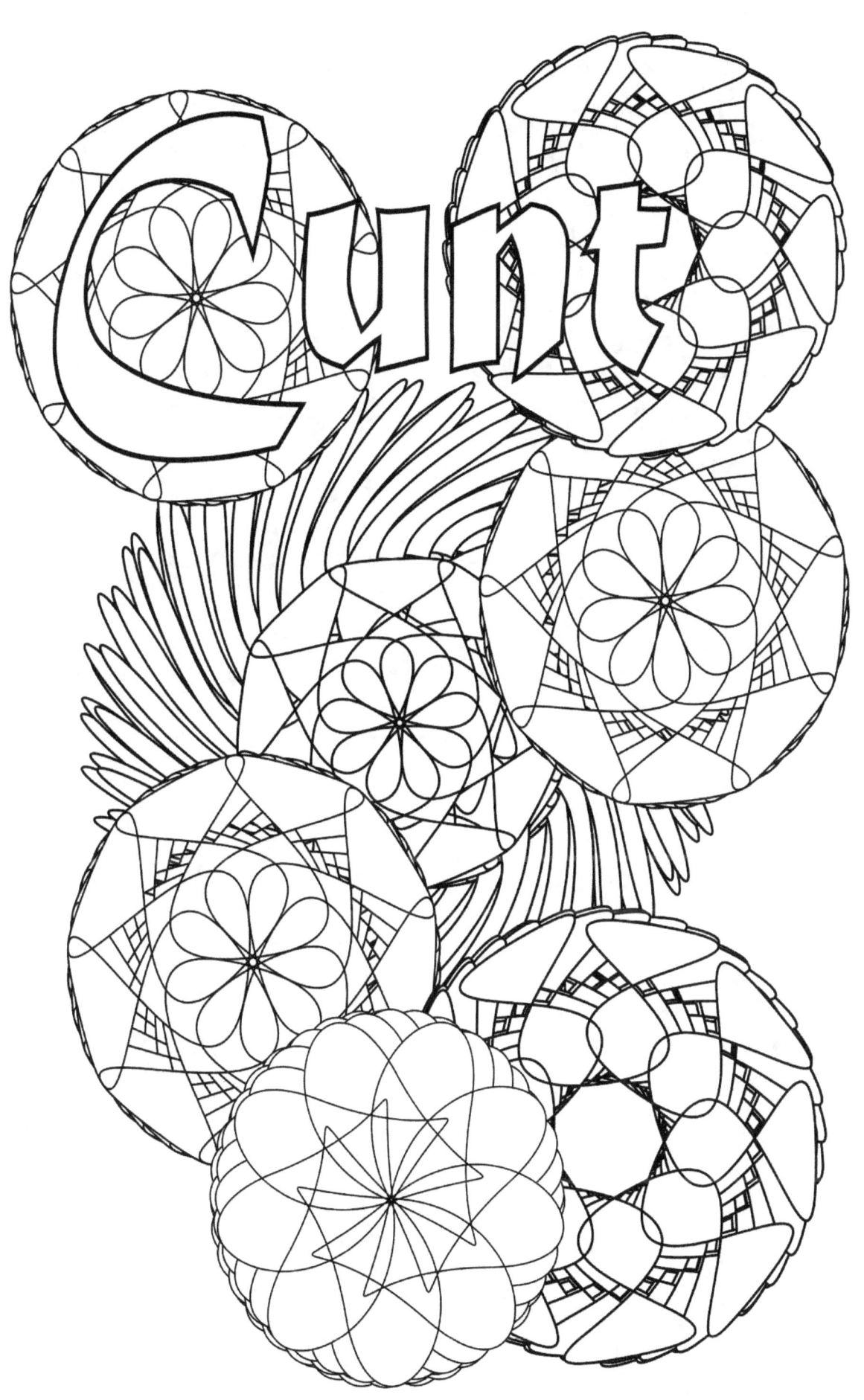

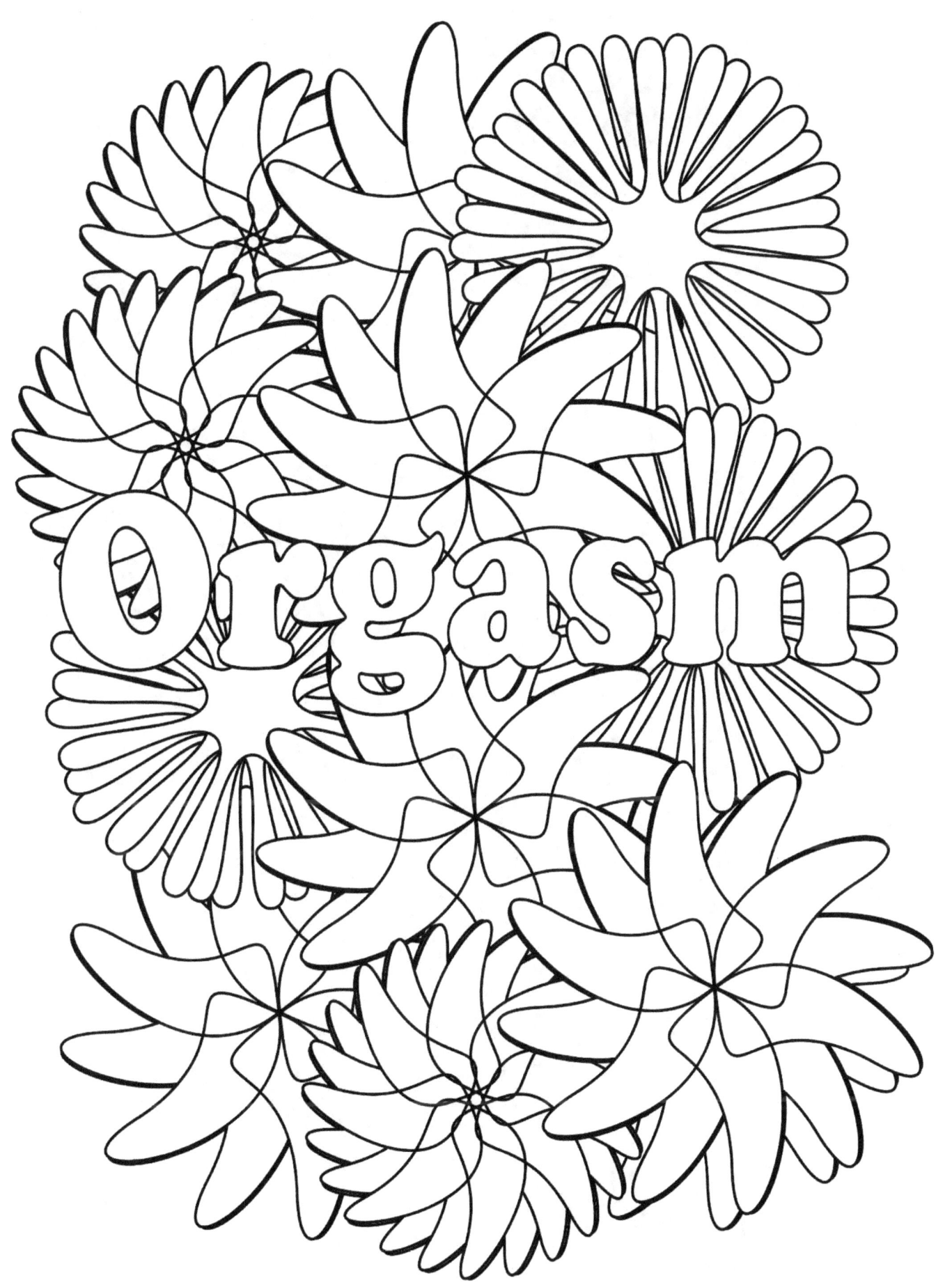

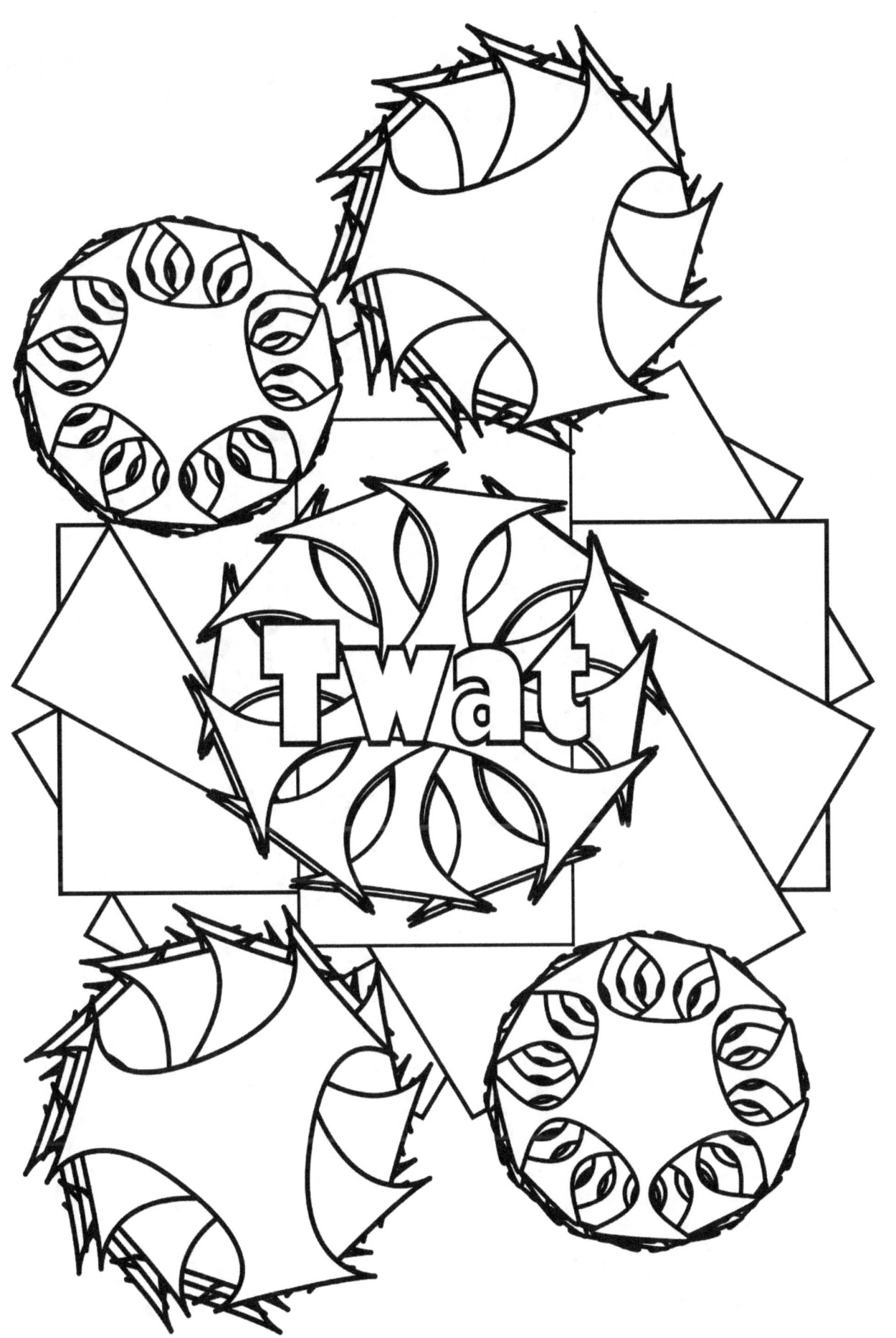

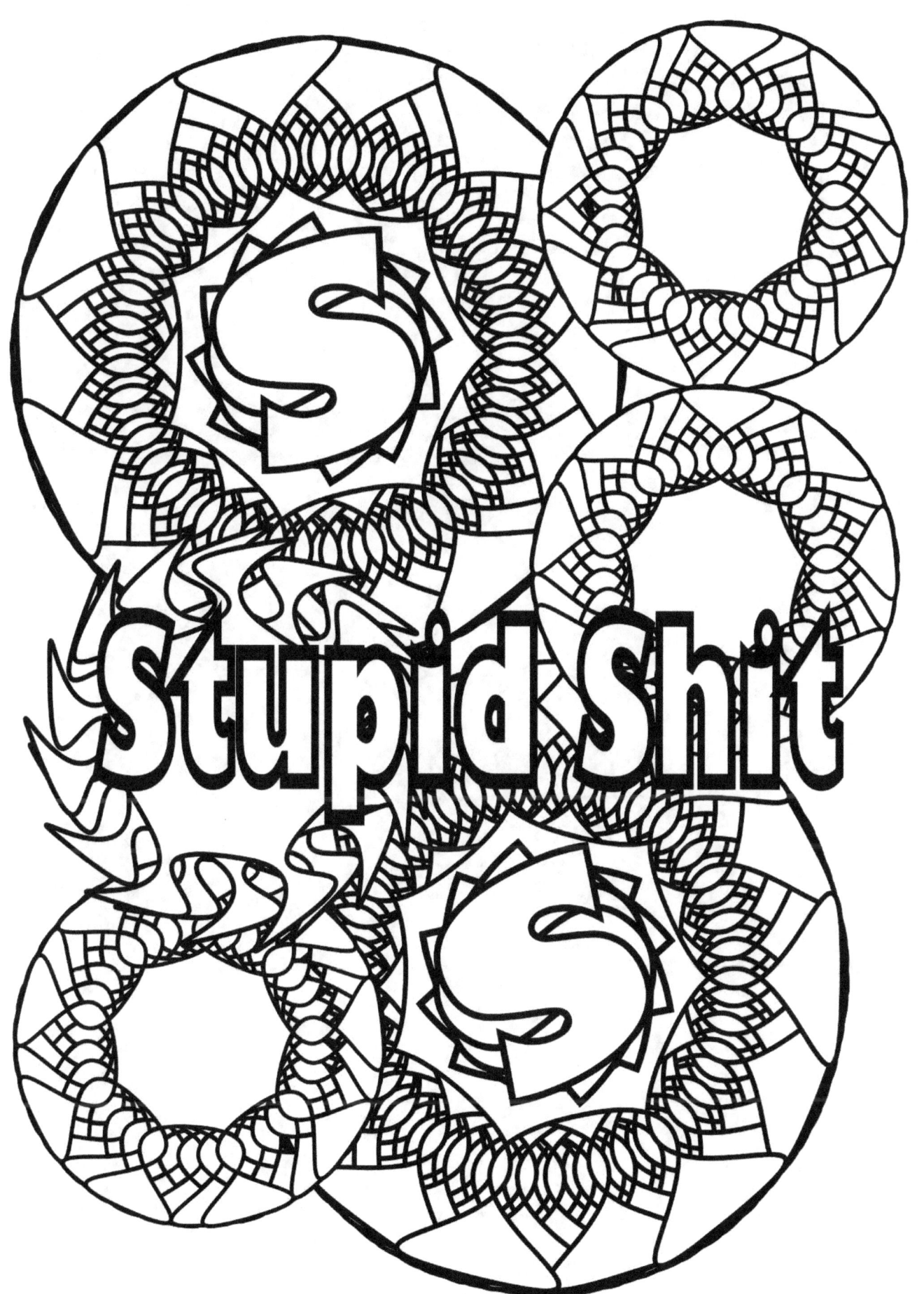

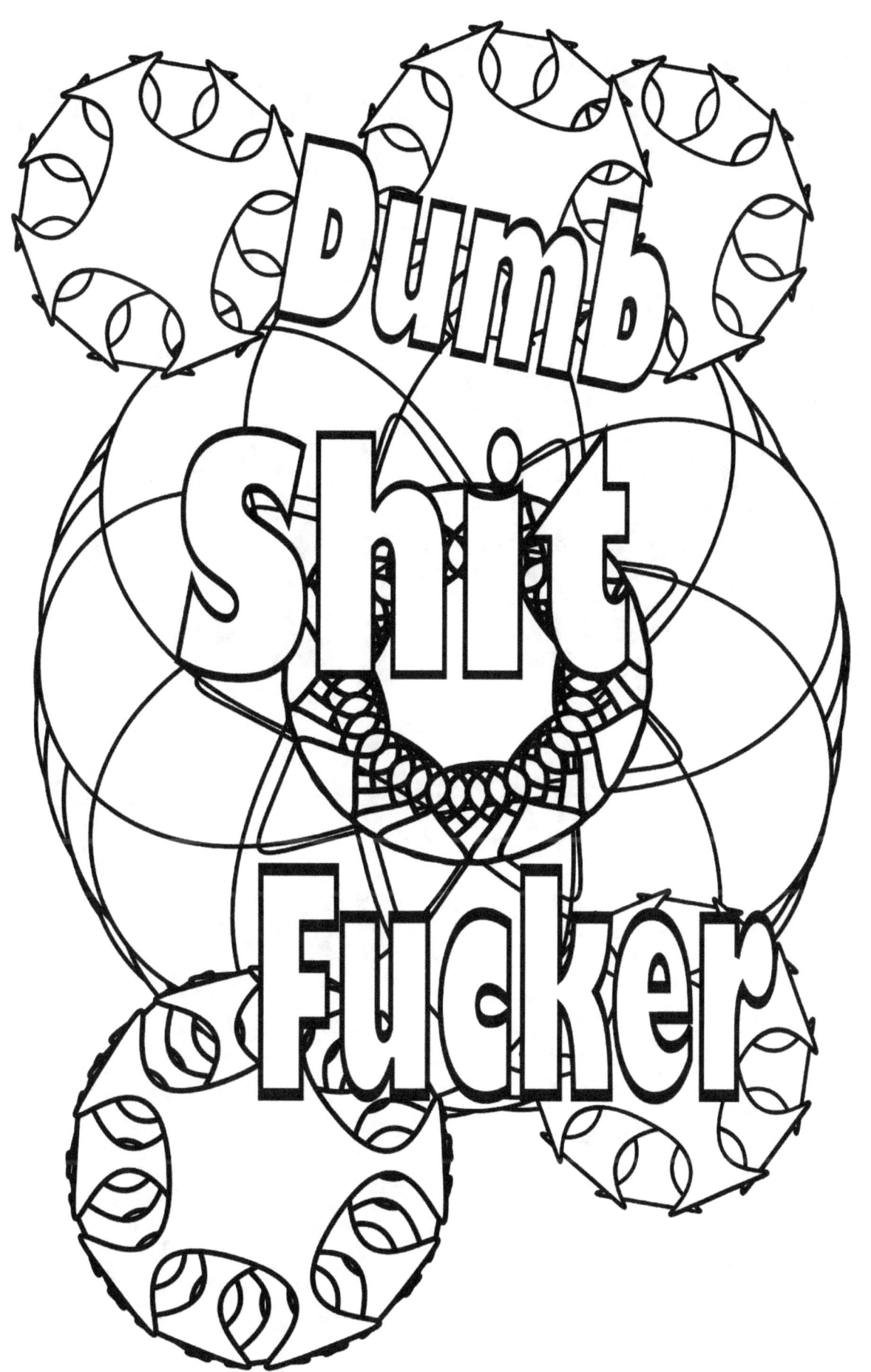

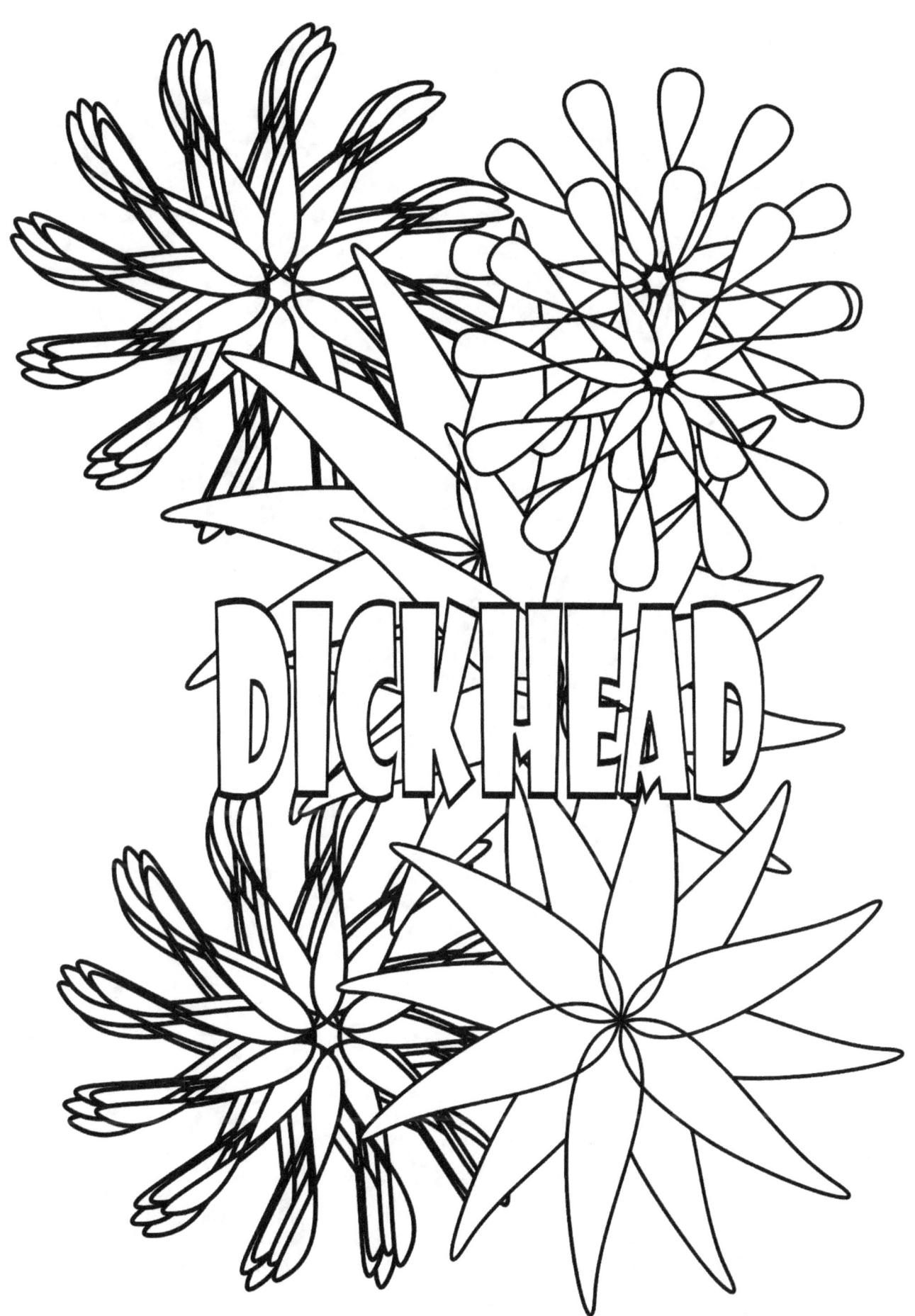

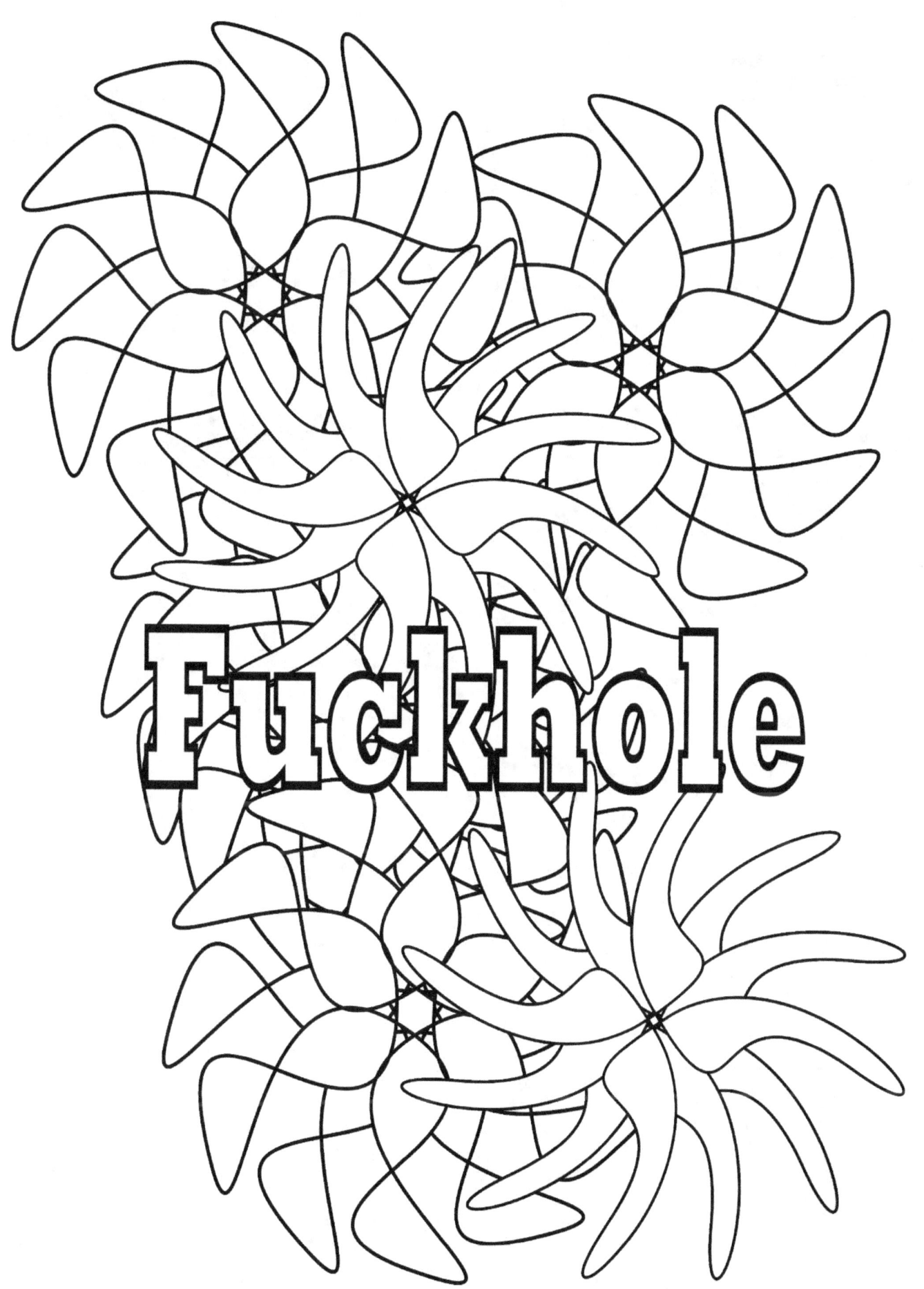

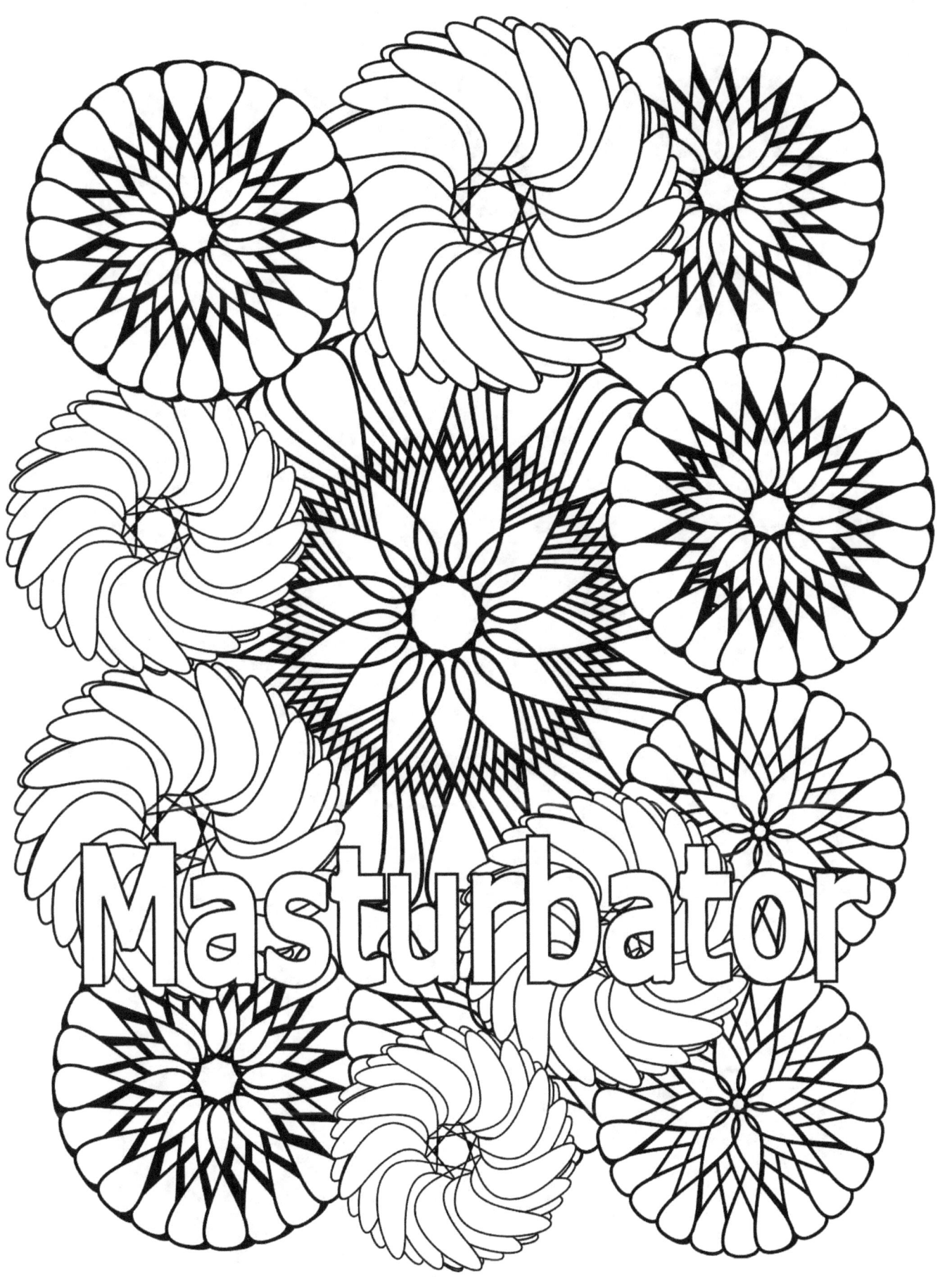

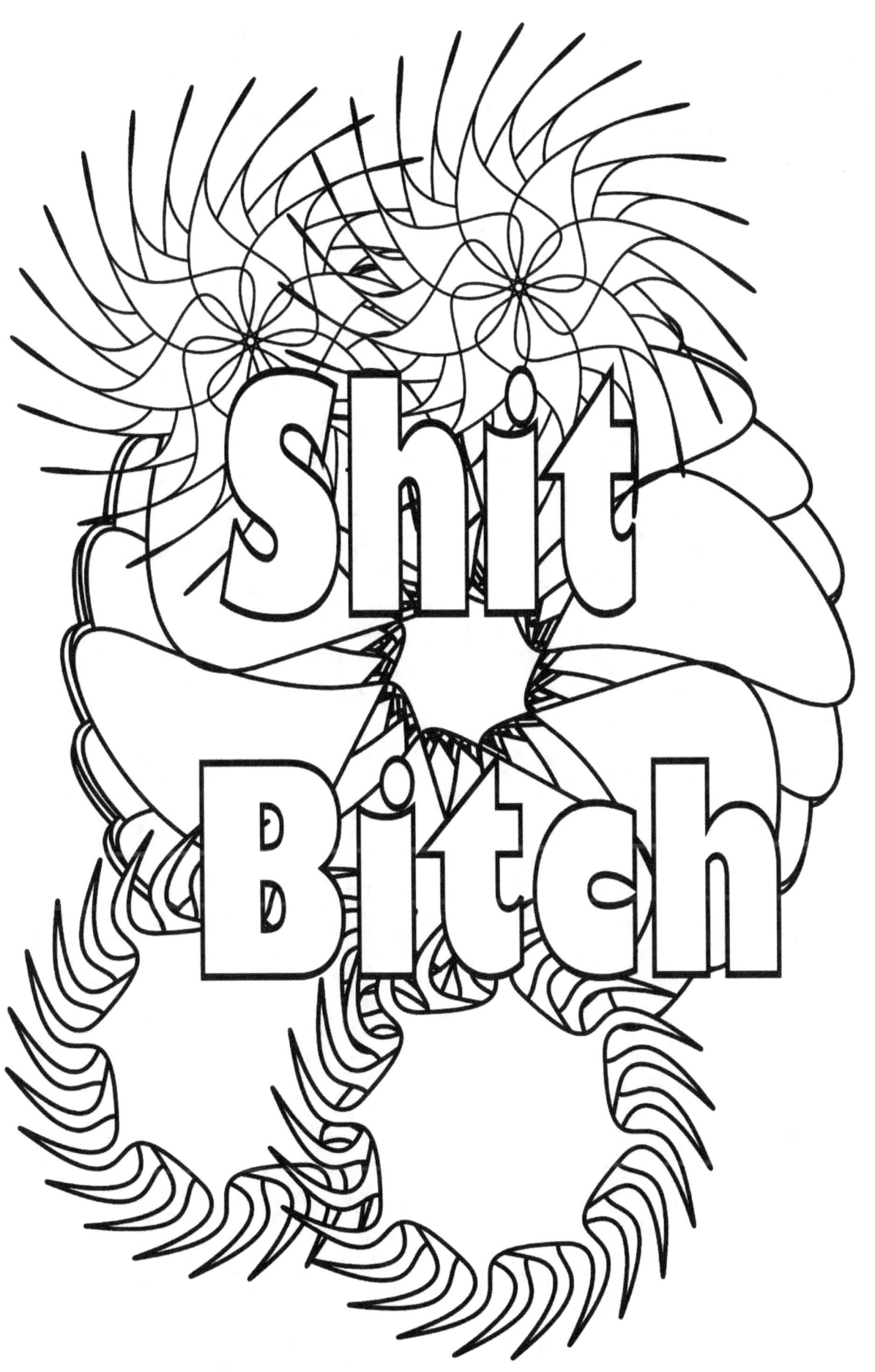

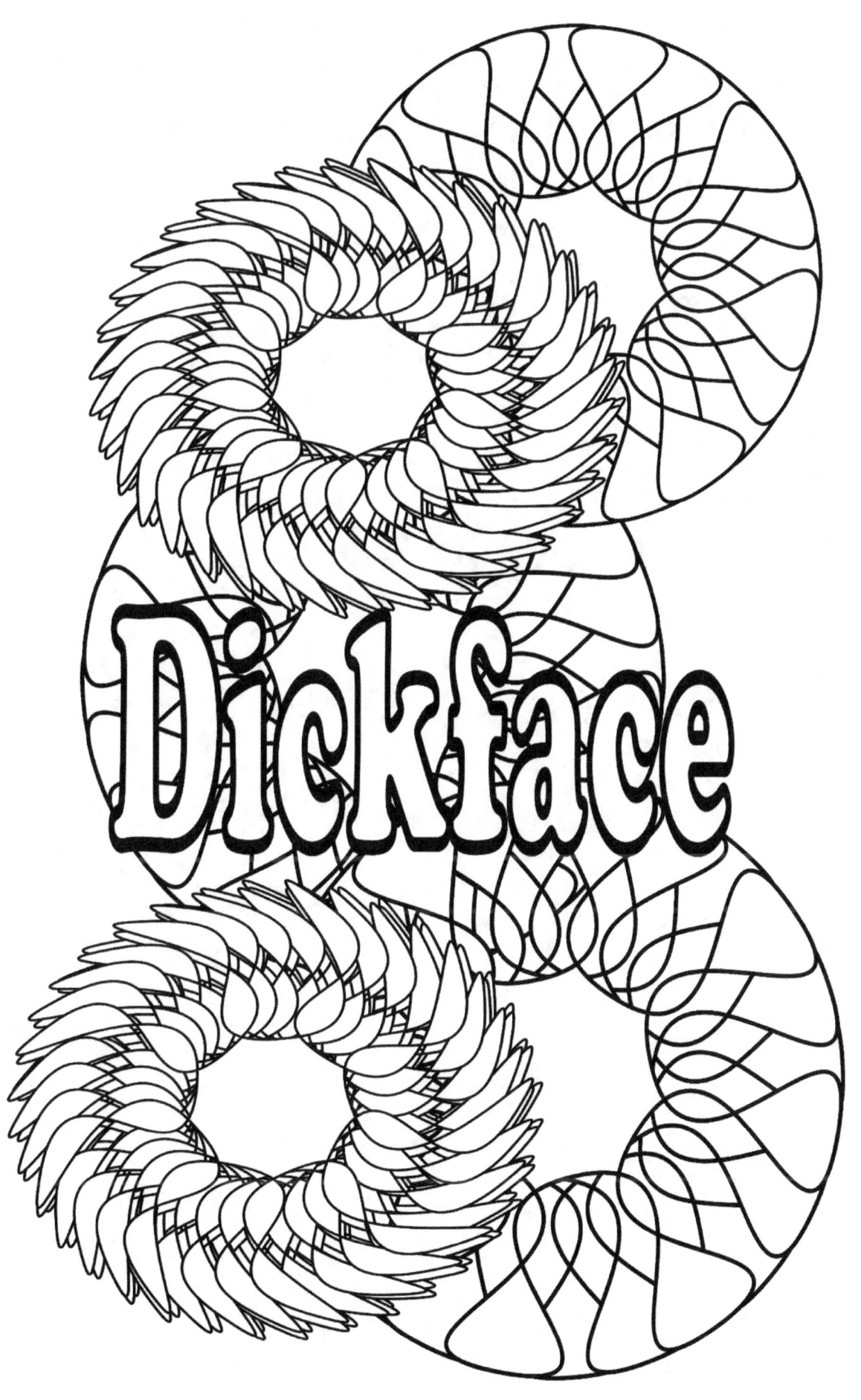

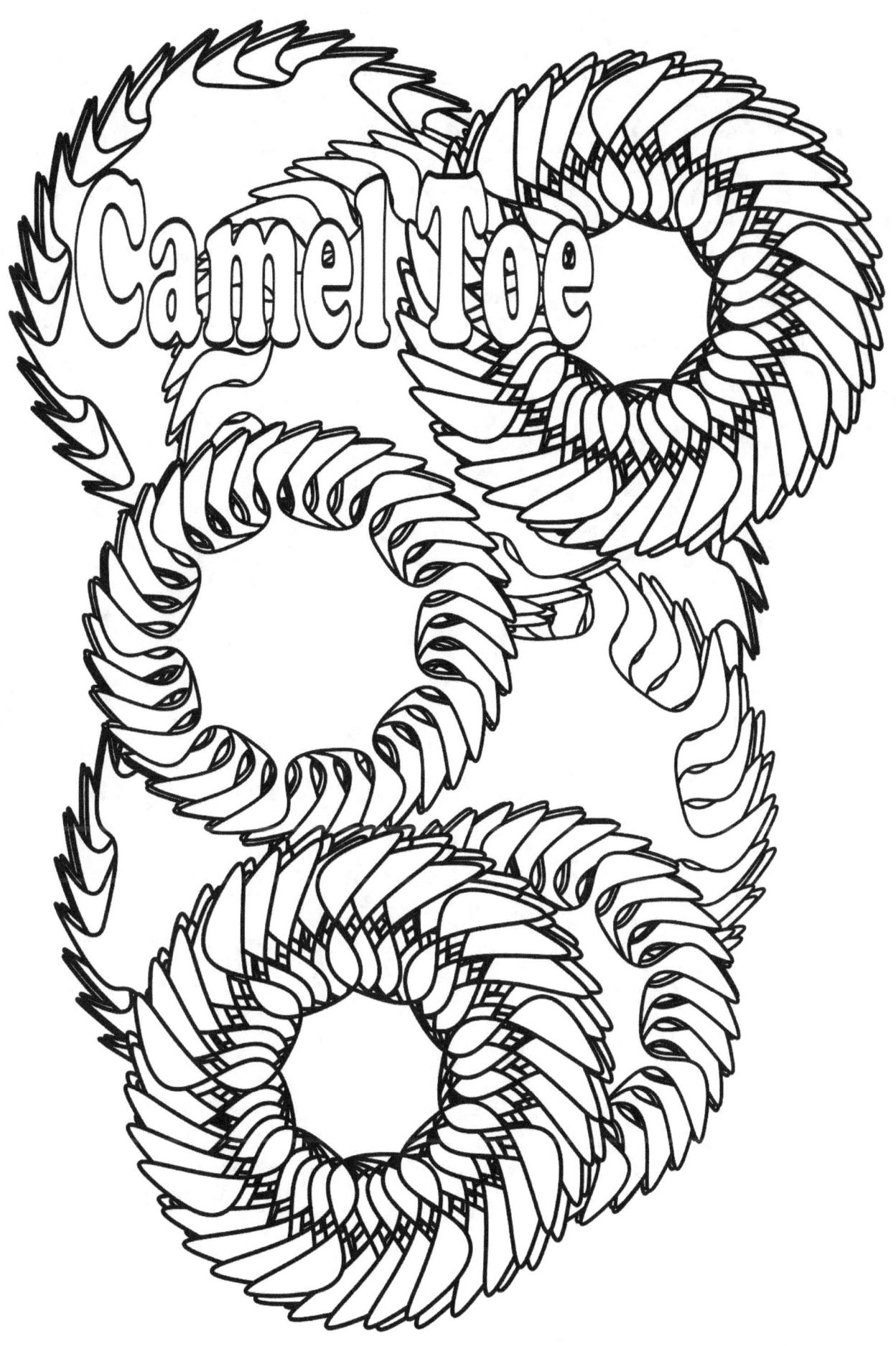

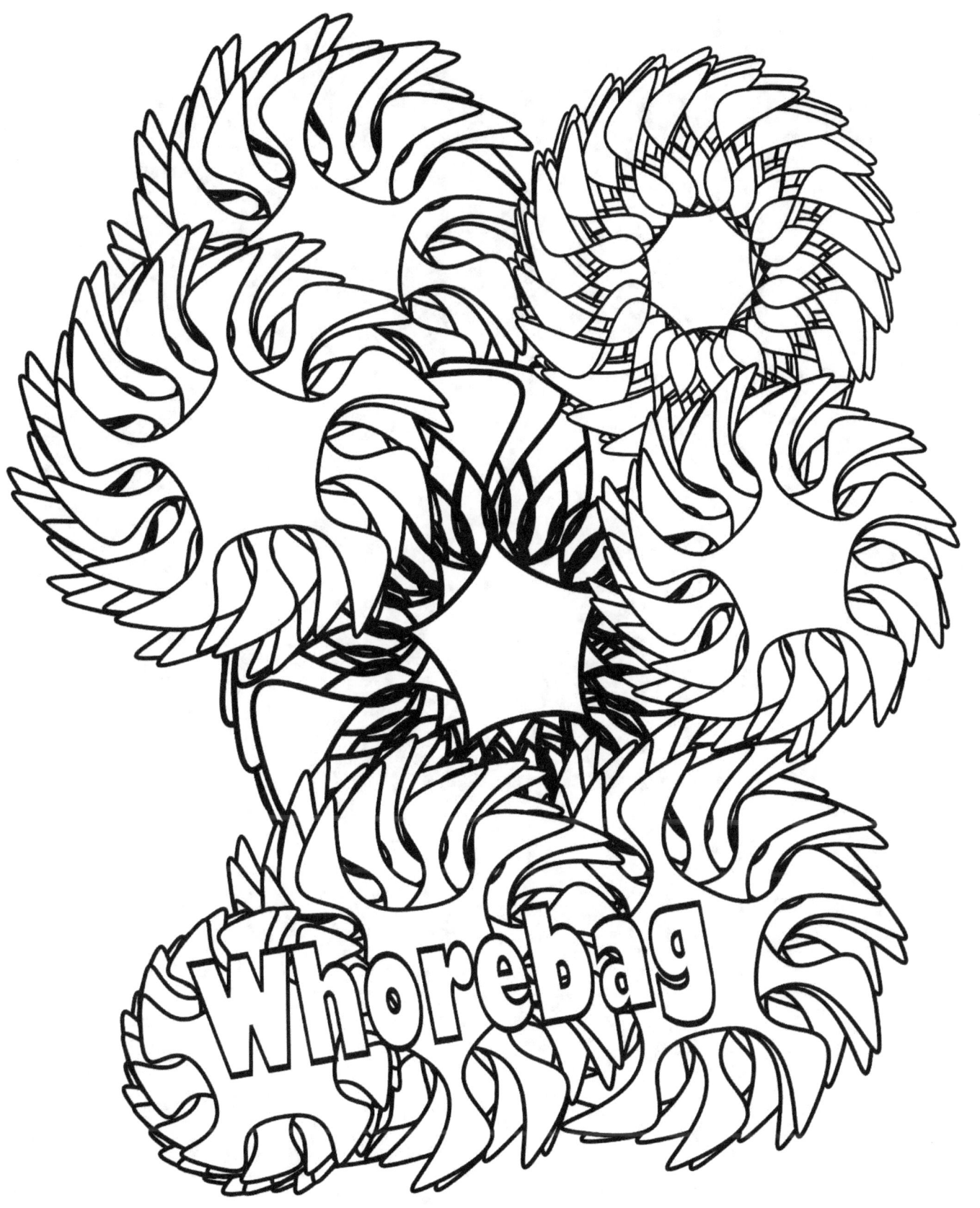

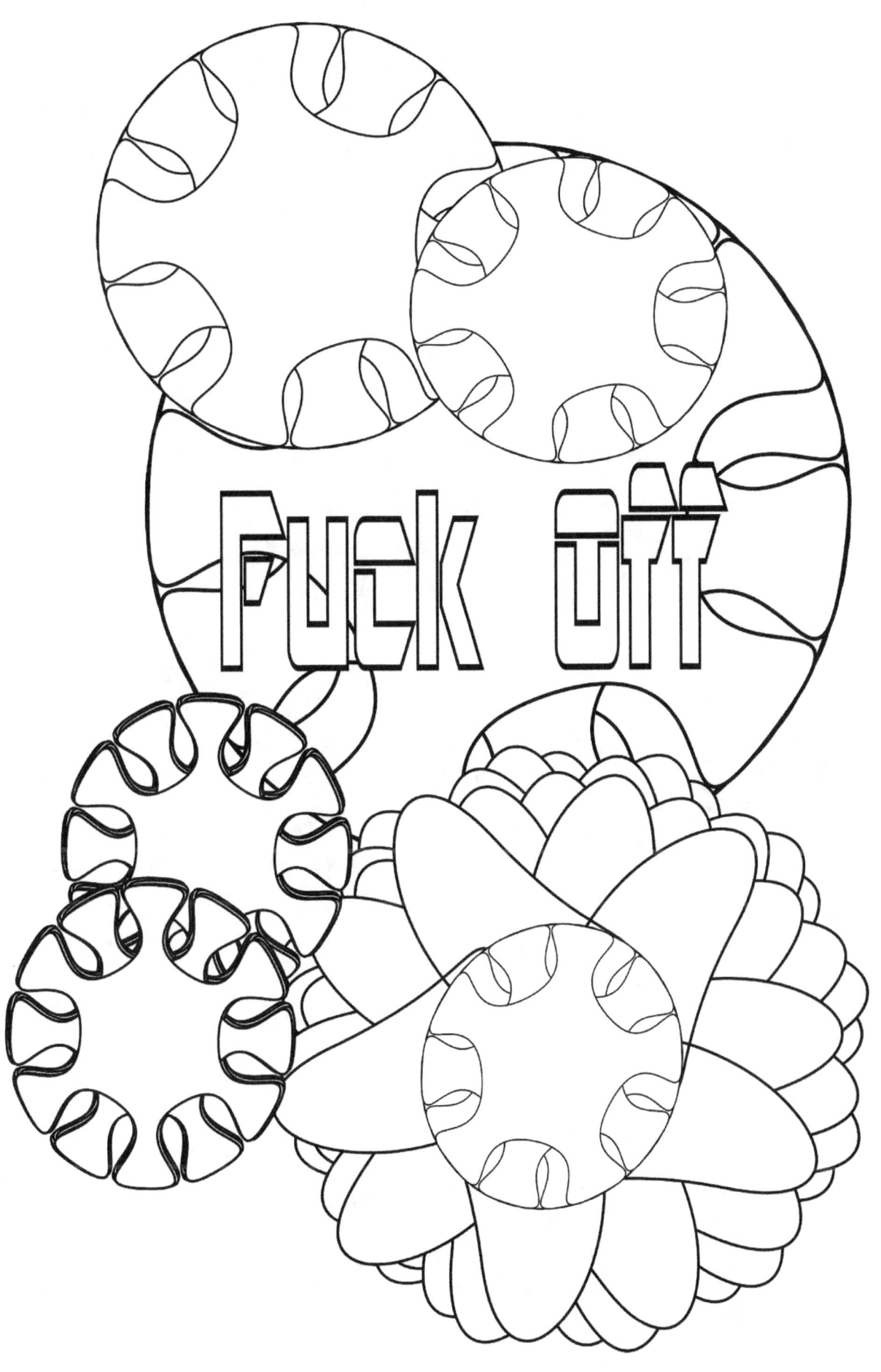

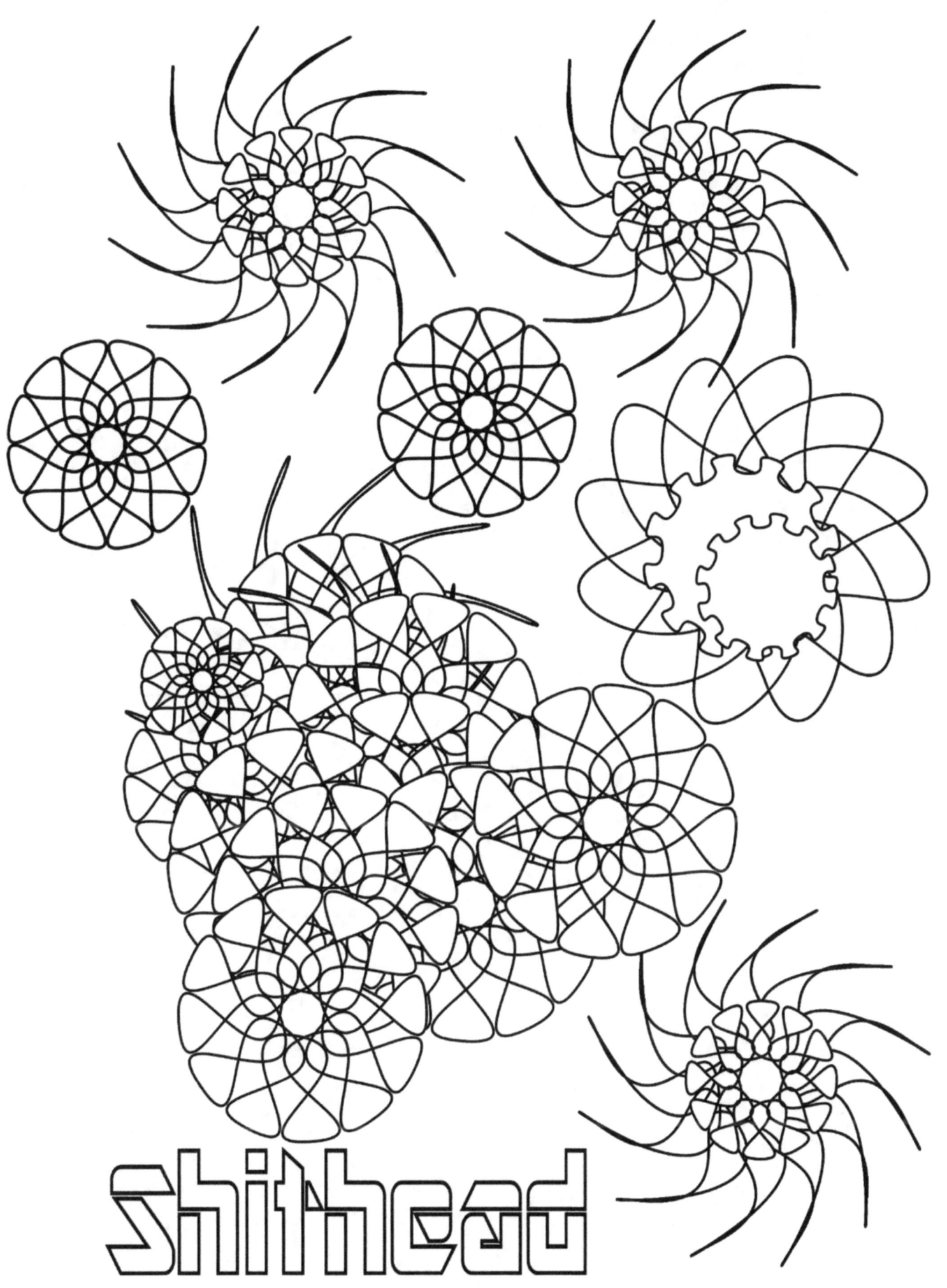

shithead

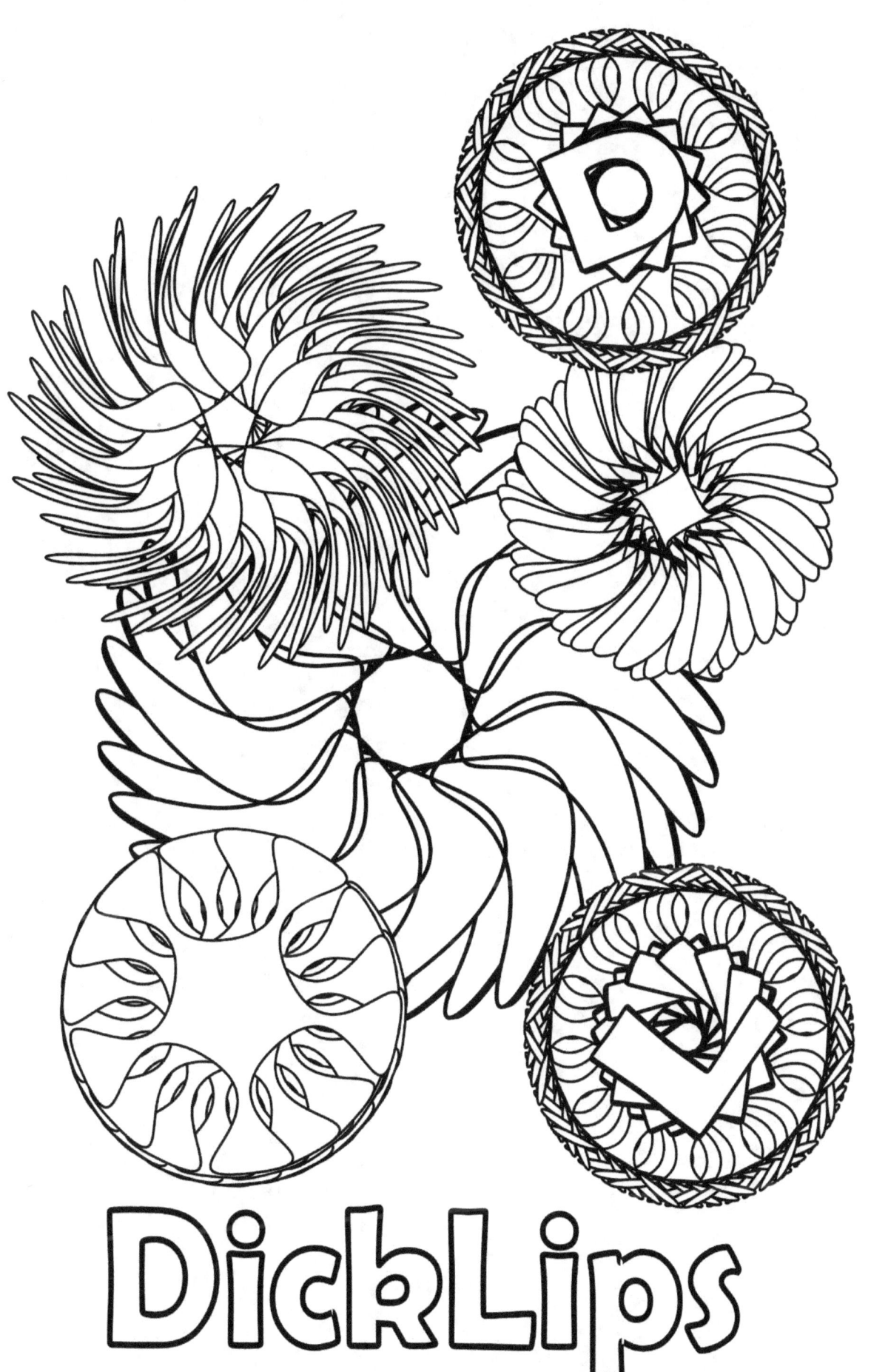

DickLips